UND~~IA AUSTRALIA~~
~~T~~ ~~Law Book Co.~~
~~Sydney~~

Carol Harlow is Emeritus Professor of Law
at the London School of Economics.

AUSTRALIA
Law Book Co.
Sydney

Canada and USA
Carswell
Toronto

HONG KONG
Sweet & Maxwell Asia

NEW ZEALAND
Brookers
Wellington

SINGAPORE and MALAYSIA
Sweet & Maxwell Asia
Singapore and Kuala Lumpur

Carol Harlow

UNDERSTANDING TORT LAW

Third Edition

LONDON
SWEET & MAXWELL
2005

Third Edition published by Sweet & Maxwell Ltd
of 100 Avenue Road, Swiss Cottage, London NW3 3PF
http://www.sweetandmaxwell.co.uk

Second Edition published by Fontana Press 1995

First Edition published in Great Britain by Fontana Press 1987

ISBN 0421 878 401

Typeset by J&L Composition, Filey, North Yorkshire

Printed in Great Britain by TJ International Ltd, Padstow, Cornwall

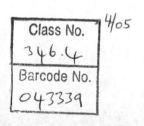

UNDERSTANDING LAW
Editor: Roger Brownsword

Understanding Law
John N. Adams and Roger Brownsword

Understanding Contract Law
John N. Adams and Roger Brownsword

Understanding Criminal Law
C.M.V. Clarkson

Understanding Public Law
Gabriele Ganz

Understanding Equity and Trusts
Jeffrey Hackney

Understanding Tort Law
Carol Harlow

Understanding Property Law
W.T. Murphy and Simon Roberts

CONTENTS

CONTENTS

PREFACE

The objective of this short book is, as the title suggests, to help its
readers understand tort law. It does not, however, set out to provide a detailed description of the principles of tort law; that is a
task for a textbook. You will find plenty of books that provide
simple and palatable accounts of tort law, some of which are
named in the Suggestions for Further Reading at the end of the
chapters or mentioned in the text. In any event, since tort law
remains very much a case law subject and has so far defied codification, an introductory text cannot hope to deal adequately with
even a small percentage of the many cases from which the principles of tort law are painfully derived. Anyone hoping to follow
this most fascinating of legal subjects further will need to read
cases and still more cases.

It would, however, be impossible to understand tort law without some knowledge of the disparate set of causes of action that
make it up. There are outlines of essential liability principles in
almost every chapter, expanded where the law is complex,
unclear or—as is too often the case—unsatisfactory. Chapter 3 in
particular is devoted to a brief account of the story of negligence,
today the "general principle of civil liability" in tort. But this book
sets out to be and is to be read primarily as a book *about* law
rather than a "law book". Its aim is to set the legal rules and principles of tort law in context by describing the way in which the
system of tort law that exists today has come about, the very dis-
similar situations in which the rules have to be applied and the
policies—or sometimes the absence of policy—which lie behind
tort law.

Because tort law remains uncodified and is to a great extent still
judge-made, its historical dimension is important in assessing the
way in which the judges will let tort law develop. A very basic historical outline and perspective on tort law's evolution is provided
in Chapter 1. Chapter 1 deals too with the relative contributions of
judges and Parliament to tort law and the relationship between
the two forms of lawmaking. Chapter 2 adopts a different and
more academic perspective on tort law. It looks at the divergent
and often conflicting theories which underlie, and frequently

complicate, judicial decision-making, tort law's objectives and the ways in which it can be used. Chapter 3, as already indicated, turns to negligence as a general principle of tortious liability. In Chapter 4, the competing notion of causation, which in practice governs the outcome of many hard cases, is dealt with separately, though the two chapters inevitably overlap.

The second section of the book deals with the way in which tort law protects specific interests, for historical reasons singled out over the centuries for judicial protection. This approach is explained more fully in Chapter 1. Chapters 5 and 6 deal with property, economic and business interests, considering reasons why they are so strongly protected and the extent to which the economic interests of a modern capitalist society are adequately looked after by the law as it has evolved.

In Chapters 7 and 8 we turn to the constitutional aspects of tort law, its traditional use for the protection of civil liberties and, currently, its growing involvement with human rights—a new entrant into the English legal order, and one which challenges the law of torts. The chapter focuses on reputation, the oldest intangible right recognised by the common law, well protected by the tort of defamation. Against this background, the reluctance of the courts to develop a law of privacy is examined, together with judicial reluctance to provide a remedy in damages for violations of human rights. This leads on to a more general discussion in Chapter 8 of the position of the State and public authorities as defendants, currently a matter of some anxiety for the judges.

In the final chapter, tort law's occasional successes and many failures are evaluated. Today nearly synonymous with personal injuries litigation, tort law must be measured against statutory accident compensation as a vehicle for redress of accident injuries. Briefly examining the possible alternatives, the book ends on a questioning note: can tort law survive?

Carol Harlow

1

WHAT IS TORT LAW?

"In most branches of English law the effect of historical accidents and procedural requirements is to obstruct orderly and scientific exposition—this is especially true of branches such as the law of torts where the sources are to be found mainly in the common law and not in statute law."

Professor Harry Street

TORT LAW AND CRIMINAL LAW

"Crime" is a word in everyday use. Newspapers are filled with reports of criminal cases and *Crimewatch* programmes absorb hours of television prime time. The word "tort", on the other hand, is something of a puzzle. It is not in common use and possesses no obvious meaning in modern English. In fact it is the French word for "wrong" and its use points us back through the centuries to the Norman French language, which was once the working language of the "King's Courts". A tort is simply a "wrong" and tort law is the law of "wrongdoing" or perhaps of "wrongs". This, however, gets us little further; indeed, it may be positively confusing. The general public tends to treat "the law" as synonymous with criminal law and it is the criminal law that is generally regarded as the law of wrongdoing. But a tort is not a criminal wrong although, as we are about to see, the two have much in common and may often overlap. Tort law establishes the circumstances in which a person whose interests have been harmed by another can be compensated through the civil courts.

But even this elementary description immediately breaks down. Tort law is only one part of what academics today prefer to call the civil law of obligations. Much of the civil law is taken up with contracts. Tort law is not in general concerned with contracts; indeed, continental lawyers often call it the "extra-contractual" law of liability. In the formative period of the nineteenth century, the line between tort and contract was seen to form the main divide in civil law. Later, Sir Percy Winfield (1931b) was to draw on this distinction, defining tort law as the breach of an obligation "imposed by the law", a definition that aligns tort and crime. In contract, which Winfield was anxious to distinguish, obligations are normally imposed by, and arise from, an agreement between the parties. When Winfield wrote, contract was the elder brother, a relationship imperceptibly undone by *Donoghue v Stevenson* (1932). Today, contract law has changed. The doctrine of privity challenged by *Donoghue* has, for example, recently been amended to allow third parties to claim limited contractual protection (Adams and Brownsword, 2004, pp.87–93). Tort law too has changed, and a new doctrine of reliance has emerged at its heart, eroding the boundary with contract (*Hedley Byrne v Heller*, 1964). Today, as the boundary line between the two has become more fluid, Winfield's definition would be thought simplistic (Cane, 1997, pp.183–186). The complex relationship between tort and contract law is, however, best reserved for later chapters.

As a way to highlight differences between criminal law and tort law, the facts of a macabre law case, which in 1990 attracted a great deal of attention in the popular press, are helpful (*Halford v Brookes*, 1991). The claimant was asking permission of the court to bring an action for damages in respect of the tragic death of her daughter more than 12 years before, in April 1978. There was no doubt that the girl had been murdered; her body was found beside a canal where she had been walking with her boyfriend, the second defendant in the civil case, then a schoolboy, and she had been both strangled and stabbed. The boy had been arrested and charged with murder and had confessed to stabbing the girl. Later, however, he withdrew this confession and made a new statement blaming his stepfather, the first defendant in this case, for the killing. At the time of the boy's trial for murder, everyone concerned, including the jury, felt confident that either he or his stepfather or both of them had been responsible for the death of the girl, yet, because the police chose to proceed only against the boy, he had to be acquitted.

Not surprisingly, the girl's family remained deeply dissatisfied. They wanted action to be taken against the stepfather and went so far as to talk to a solicitor, who told them that only the Director of Public Prosecutions could take action. With the help of local people and the press, they mounted a sustained campaign to persuade the authorities to act but, despite the emergence of new evidence, nothing was done. In 1985, the mother consulted new solicitors who came up with a novel idea. Advising that a case in the civil courts might be a possibility, they applied successfully for legal aid to start proceedings against both of the men involved. After some preliminaries, the case went to a High Court judge for trial. In a judgment that attracted much press attention, the judge ruled that the stepfather was 100 per cent liable in damages for the acts of strangulation and stabbing. The stepson was held to have participated to a limited extent in the stabbing and was held liable to make a 20 per cent contribution to the damages. Justice had at last been done. Or had it? Crime and punishment are, after all, indelibly linked in the public mind, yet here no one had been punished.

A counter-reason why the procedure used in *Halford* can seem unjust is that a man, who had not been charged and did not actually participate in the civil proceedings, had effectively been found "guilty" of murder by a single judge in a case that ought normally to have come before a jury. Jury trial is an ancient right, which can be traced back to Magna Carta in 1215 and forms a central part of our constitutional guarantees. In Britain, though not in the United States, juries have gone out of use in all but exceptional civil cases, which significantly include those where police wrongdoing is alleged. All serious criminal charges are still heard with juries, however. Again, because criminal prosecutions carry the risk of loss of liberty, the burden of proof in a criminal case lies on the prosecution to prove guilt "beyond all reasonable doubt". In a civil case, which could never result in imprisonment, the burden lies on the claimant to prove the case to the lighter standard of "balance of probabilities". The trial judge in *Halford* showed some sensitivity to the constitutional position by applying both the criminal standard of proof and the rules of evidence used in criminal trials to the case before declaring himself satisfied.

Criminal cases involve a relationship between the state and the individual, with the state or Crown representing the public interest. In *Halford* we should notice that the case was not brought in the name of the Crown or by the prosecuting authorities; indeed, it was a way to challenge their failure to act against the stepfather. Until the nineteenth century, the responsibility to prosecute criminals normally fell on individuals. They still possess the right to prosecute and still occasionally do so; a private prosecution for corporate manslaughter was brought after the tragic Zeebrugge disaster, when a cross-Channel ferry capsized (*R. v Stanley*, 1990). A notoriously unsuccessful private prosecution was brought after the infamous murder of Stephen Lawrence, where nobody was satisfactorily brought to justice and a public inquiry had to be held (Cm.4262–I, 1999). But the Attorney-General, exercising an ancient Crown prerogative, can always withdraw a prosecution, even one started by a private citizen. In contrast, a civil action, brought by an individual, can be "struck out" by the court only if the judge believes that no good cause of action exists. Normally, the decision to prosecute is taken by the Crown Prosecution Service, set up by the Police and Criminal Evidence Act 1984 to supply an element of objectivity in criminal proceedings, and CPS lawyers, headed by an independent Director of Public Prosecutions, take charge of the proceedings. Here we have another difference with the tort action, which is run by the individual claimant and her lawyers. This is an important feature of tort law, which allows it to be used for purposes of accountability. In contrast, the distance between the public and criminal prosecutions has widened to the point that a strong victims' lobby is demanding a more responsive criminal justice system, with rights for victims and their relatives to express their views. Victims' groups are today routinely consulted by the Home Office, which has introduced many changes to make criminal procedure victim-friendly. The new practices blur the crime/tort distinction, bringing crime and tort closer together.

Different courts, presided over by different judges and magistrates, handle criminal and civil cases. Since 1973, however, criminal courts have been empowered to order convicted offenders to pay compensation to their victim in addition to any criminal penalty imposed. Even when, as is normally the case for minor offences, punishment takes the form of a fine, the fine is not payable to the victim; currently, around 4 per cent of fined offenders make some compensation to their victim. Typically, the sum awarded is small; in magistrates' courts, where most compensation orders are made, awards average £144; in Crown Courts, £1,444. This is partly because magistrates tend to see compensation orders as double punishment, partly because in criminal proceedings the means of the convicted person must be considered so that full compensation may not be forthcoming. A criminal compensation order does not bar civil proceedings, although the same sum cannot be recovered twice over.

The outcome of a successful tort action is an award of "damages" or sum of money awarded as compensation and, in civil proceedings, the means of the defendant are not relevant either to liability or to calculation of damages. The rules for calculating civil damages are both complicated and controversial and this book will not deal with them in any detail, but the basic principle should be borne in mind: this is that the claimant's injuries are to be redressed or repaired *in full*. It is perfectly possible, though uncommon, for the victim of crime to sue the criminal for damages, but the criminal is not usually worth suing; he is often behind bars or his earnings may be insufficient to compensate the victim and to pay the legal costs. The Home Office is anxious, however, to make criminals contribute more to the costs of compensation. Early in 2004 it issued a consultation paper, *Compensation and Support for Victims of Crime* recommending changes to the system to make it on the one hand more victim-friendly and, on the other, to make the criminal pay. Once again, crime and tort are coming closer together.

Even if the outcome of a successful tort action is an award of "damages", we would be cynical to believe the mother in *Halford* was interested in money as "compensation" for loss of her daughter; indeed, the trial judge went out of his way to note her real motive as being to target and expose the stepfather, whom she believed to be "the primary, and perhaps only, author of her daughter's death". If money had been the claimant's main objective, the state-funded criminal injuries compensation scheme (see below, p.158) would be a better source than the two impecunious defendants against whom the award was made. In fact *Halford* exemplifies the growing use of tort law for purposes of accountability and even revenge, a development further discussed in Ch.2. Once again, the line between crime and tort is blurred. Damages were claimed to compensate for loss of the daughter's earnings up until the date of the trial, an amount roughly calculable, as well as for her "loss of expectation of life", a guess rather than a calculation. In addition, a claim for "aggravated damages" was added, defined recently by the Law Commission as an award to "compensate for mental distress caused by the manner or motive with which the wrong was committed" (Law Com.247, 1997).

It is really more honest to retain the traditional idea as expressed by Lord Hailsham in *Broome v Cassell* (1972) that aggravated damages, like punitive and exemplary damages, are all awarded in exceptional circumstances to express the public's "indignation at the excessive nature of treatment meted out to the plaintiff". While these categories remain in being, the division between tort and criminal law is incomplete.

DEFINING TORT LAW

If we are by now beginning to have some idea of what tort law is *not*, we are not much nearer to knowing what it is. This is because, two or more centuries after tort law emerged as a discrete subject and the first tort textbook was written, no rational and logical definition has yet been provided; indeed, argument still rages over whether there is any such thing as "tort law". Some authors still follow Sir John Salmond, one of the subject's greatest scholars, in talking of "the law of torts". This implies that tort law remains "a body of rules establishing specific injuries", unco-ordinated by general principles (Salmond and Heuston, 1992, p.14). In contrast, Sir Percy Winfield, who saw negligence as a unifying thread for tort law, chose to call his textbook *The Law of Tort* (Winfield and Jolowicz).

Some modern authors have attempted to identify tort law's essential elements and reclassify the law around them. Professor Harry Street (1983, p.5), for example, identified as issues common to all tort actions three basic questions:

- What interests does the law of torts protect?

- Against what general type of conduct—malicious, intentional, negligent, or accidental—are these interests protected?

- Is there some special circumstance that provides a defence?

Street's analysis correctly depicts tort law as a balancing exercise, in which the court weighs the claimant's protected interest against the defendant's breach of obligation; it does not tell us what interests are protected or what the defendant's obligations are. Cane (1997, p.1) also depicts tort law in terms of three main components: a protected interest; conduct that the law sanctions; and a remedy for the "wrong". He sets out to "dismantle" tort law and reconstruct it as a "system of ethical rules and principles of personal responsibility for conduct". But Cane is unable to provide a rational definition, concluding that tort law should be "discarded as a category with juridical significance" (Cane, 1997, p.238). This book, like Cane and Street, focuses on the idea of protected interests but, like them too, it cannot move far from the laundry list of torts.

These somewhat abstract points are illustrated by a final look back at *Halford*. This case revolved around an unsuccessful charge of murder, a crime with which we are all familiar and the meaning of which we probably understand. We might reasonably expect the elements of the crime of murder to be replicated in the civil law of tort. Let us test this expectation by guessing at the answer to Street's three questions:

- Yes, the law of torts protects physical integrity, including no doubt the fundamental right to life.

- Life and physical integrity are sufficiently important to be protected against malicious, intentional and negligent acts. This raises the question whether liability for unintentional or accidental acts is excluded or whether someone is "strictly liable" for deaths which he has caused;

- There might be special circumstances—like necessity or self-defence—that provide defences, as there are in criminal law.

Following logical principles, we have concluded that murder, or causing death intentionally, must be an actionable civil law wrong or tort. The fact is, however, that "causing death" is not, for historical reasons, an actionable wrong. Although we do not want to go too deeply into the reasons, some explanation of such a surprising gap in the civil law is appropriate. The difficulty springs from two interlinked common law rules of great antiquity, which locked together to preclude actions founded on someone's death:

- Rule I was procedural in character: it provided that no personal actions survived the death of the plaintiff or defendant, which meant that the executors of the estate of a deceased person (like Mrs Halford) could not sue in the name of the deceased person;

- Rule II provided that no action lay for loss to third parties caused through someone's death. This rule prevented the widow, children or other dependants from suing where the family breadwinner had been killed. The rule was confirmed in the case of *Baker v Bolton* (1808), unfortunately decided slightly before industrialisation and railway accidents began causing anxiety about compensation for the dependents of accident victims.

The crime of murder therefore has no exact equivalence in civil law. How was this problem to be overcome in *Halford*? The term "murder" was replaced in the civil proceedings by use of the ancient generic tort of *trespass to the person*, obsolete except in the language of the law and of the prayer book and again merely meaning "wrong". A trespass is an intentional or deliberate act causing physical harm. Force actually used against the person is a *battery*; to threaten force is *assault*. These "nominate torts" are some of the earliest wrongs for which the common law granted redress. The modern reader is likely to be more comfortable with the principled, theoretical approaches of Street and Cane. Instead we find that a list of causes of action or nominate torts is an essential addition to the more theoretical approaches.

Perhaps all this does not greatly matter. Perhaps we have to accept that, in a common law system, the only way to track down our subject is to turn to the index of a standard textbook, where the chapter headings will provide a number of clues. Sir Frederick Pollock, another great legal scholar, once observed, "There is rather too much talk about definitions. A definition, strictly speaking, is nothing but an abbreviation in which the user of the term defined may please himself." (Pollock, 1931, p.588) If the traditional "formulaic" approach cannot answer the anguished question, "What is tort law?" it can at least provide answers to the question, "What is a tort?" Yet it remains an unsatisfactory answer (Cane, 1997, pp.1–10; Murphy, 1999, p.116). Due to the lack of any central organising principle, tort law ebbs and flows in a painfully unstructured and unprincipled fashion, with little agreement over its parameters and even less over its functions and objectives. It is still governed at the start of the twenty-first century by ancient and often obsolete forms of action into which, we are told, the facts of any given case have to be fitted if the claimant is to succeed. As the celebrated legal historian, Sir Frederic Maitland, famously remarked, "We have buried the forms of action but they still rule us from their graves".

THE COMMON LAW AND CODIFICATION

The forms of action were in fact buried by the Common Law Procedure Act 1852, which made it unnecessary to refer to a specific form of action in one's pleadings. In 1873 the Supreme Court Judicature Act finally abolished the forms of action for all procedural purposes. It was, generally speaking, no longer necessary to pigeonhole one's claim within a cause of action, but simply to set out the facts on which one's claim was based. This necessary reform took the bones out of the ancient common law system.

The easiest way to put them back would have been for Parliament to codify the common law along the lines of the French Civil Code introduced by Napoleon in 1806. This compresses the general principles of tort or "delict"—another word for wrong—into five articles. The two key articles provide:

Article 1382
Every act which causes damage to another person obliges the person by whose fault the damage has been caused to provide reparation.

Article 1383
A person is responsible for the damage which has been caused not only by his own acts, but also through his negligence or imprudence.

The French Civil Code has been criticised by a modern German scholar for reducing the law of delict to "a handful of majestic if trivial propositions", which do no more than act as pointers to the way in which judges should develop the law (Kötz, 1987). The Code is no more than a set of "principles" or even "standards", so general as to leave everything to judicial discretion. In fact this reflects the way in which courts typically formulate their rulings. (Compare Art.1382 with the famous "neighbour" principle enunciated by Lord Atkin in *Donoghue* (see below, p.48), which forms the basis of negligence liability in modern English law.) How do judges apply principles to specific cases? And how do they fill in gaps left by general principle? Cautious by temperament and trained to reason by reference to decided cases, they look at decided cases and turn back to the law as it existed prior to codification or legislation. In other words, in a common law system, the case law always provides the context for legislation and remains in existence except insofar as Parliament has provided otherwise. In a common law system, the common law might in the same way be seen to form the essential background to a code.

It is in many ways surprising that English law escaped codification in the nineteenth century. The idea was certainly fashionable amongst intellectuals such as Jeremy Bentham, who believed that the law ought to be codified to lessen the judges' grip over it. Had his suggestion been taken up, however, a very different code would probably have resulted. More in tune stylistically with British thinking is the nineteenth-century Criminal Code published in 1877 by Sir James Stephen, never enacted as law inside the United Kingdom, although it became the basis for penal codes throughout the British empire. This relatively long and detailed text starts by enunciating general principles of liability and goes on to list and define specific offences.

Although tort law has never been codified, there is a limited amount of statutory intervention, much of which today emanates from the Law Commission. The Law Commission was set up in 1965 "to keep the law of England and Wales under review and to recommend reform when it is needed". In practice, however, the Government often commissions Law Commission reports. A good example of the English method of codification in operation is the Animals Act 1971. This Act, fairly typical of British legislative practice, set out to codify the common law rules of civil liability for damage caused by animals. It is based on a Report and Draft Bill from the Law Commission (Law Com.13, 1967), though Parliament did not accept the draft in its entirety. It is notable that there is no statement of general principle approximating to Art.1382 of the French Civil Code in the Act. Instead, the Animals Act takes as its point of departure the messy and unprincipled common law. It singles out for abolition certain common law rules that impose strict liability for wild animals deemed to be ferocious and also the archaic "action on the case" for "cattle trespass", but closely follows the existing law by retaining the crucial common law distinction between wild animals belonging to a dangerous species, such as tigers and lions, and domestic animals, deemed harmless unless the contrary has been shown (the so-called "one bite" rule). With the following formula, s.8(1) altered the old rules concerning the escape of animals on to the highway:

"So much of the rules of the common law relating to liability for negligence as excludes or restricts the duty which a person might owe to others to take such care as is reasonable to see that damage is not caused by animals straying on to a highway is hereby abolished."

This is a far cry from the French Civil Code. Not only is it hard to see precisely what has been abolished but also the section does not clearly tell us what principle of liability applies. Indirectly, it is clear that negligence is somehow relevant but we cannot know until the judges tell us whether nominate torts or areas of strict liability are still applicable. The position is made more difficult by the fact that s.5, described by Lord Denning M.R. as "very cumbrously worded" and likely to give rise to difficulties in the future, sets out exceptions to strict liability.

Shortly after legislating, Parliament chose to return to the topic with the Guard Dogs Act 1975, which makes it a minor criminal offence to let a guard dog run loose in the absence of a handler. Two further Dangerous Dogs Acts followed in 1989 and 1991, the first of which started life as a Private Member's Bill. They also deal with criminal liability for dogs of a specially dangerous species, such as ridgebacks or rottweilers, when kept as pets. Instead of a codification, we have now arrived at a situation where the criminal and civil liability of the keeper of a dog is dealt with separately and two Acts contain rules on the circumstances in which dogs can be destroyed: there are powers to order the destruction of dogs that have molested humans in the Dangerous Dogs Acts, but dogs found worrying livestock are dealt with by the Animals Act. These patches have made the law very complex: the rules of criminal and civil law differ, while the classification into dangerous and non-dangerous animals is inconsistent.

Unfortunately, the habit of "law reform by penny numbers" is typical of the uncodified, common law method. The Law Commission is sometimes unsufficiently courageous; its reports stay too close to the common law. On the other hand, legislation is often far too specific. It fails to sweep up and codify related statutory provisions and to abolish the surrounding common law once and for all. Perhaps we should regret the fact that Bentham and Stephen were not Napoleon.

THE ERA OF FAULT

At the end of the eighteenth century, the forms of action, a set of disparate wrongs grouped around protected interests, notably personal physical integrity, land and property, were still in place. In the nineteenth century, the system of forms of action was partly dismantled but not entirely disposed of. Law reform converged with events taking place externally in society to change the picture and foster the development of a new law of torts based firmly on the general principle of fault (White, 1980, pp.13–19). The Industrial Revolution was under way. The rapid development of railways and industrialisation of the work force led to multiple accidents for which some reparation seemed necessary. Thus, in 1846, Lord Campbell, worried about the increase in railway accidents and the failure of the common law to acknowledge a right of action in respect of death, introduced a Death by Accident Compensation Bill into the House of Lords. Despite his fear that his bill would be defeated in the House of Commons by the strong railway lobby, it survived to become the Fatal Accidents Act 1846. Lord Campbell's Act, still virtually intact in an amended form, allowed dependants (the wife, husband, parent or child) to bring an independent action in tort in respect of their financial dependency on a person whose death the defendant had caused. It was thus of great importance in securing compensation in cases of fatal accident.

As already suggested, parliamentary intervention of this type was unusual. Parliament did not authorise the courts to depart radically from common law and gave no broad pointers to the judiciary, as Napoleon in his Civil Code had tried to do, as to how they were to develop the "law of torts". The judges therefore had to continue to operate within the framework of the old rules. Fortunately, a new profession of academic law was emerging. The new professors saw their vocation as being to expound the law systematically and coherently, reducing the common law to an orderly series of principles (Sugarman, 1986). They set out to reclassify the common law, abandoning the old compartments formed by the forms of action and choosing instead to mark out boundaries between criminal law, contract and "torts". New textbooks exemplified these objectives and in 1887, Sir Frederick Pollock published the first treatise on the law of torts. Suddenly, the intellectual climate seemed right for the emergence of negligence.

Fault law seemed just to nineteenth-century lawyers because it fitted comfortably inside both the prevailing moral and economic philosophies. The American judge, Oliver Wendell Holmes, defends fault liability in his treatise on the common law in terms of a moral argument based on fairness: it is "only just to give a man a fair chance to avoid doing the harm before he is held responsible for it" (Holmes, 1906, p.50). But Holmes also expresses clear preferences for economic laissez-faire and state inaction and these views were widespread at the time within the legal profession and judiciary (Halliday and Karpik, 1997). It has been argued that fault liability in the nineteenth century operated as a hidden subsidy to industry. Because the burden of proof in negligence rested on the claimant and because of the very restricted scope of vicarious liability, the employer seldom had to pay the true costs of his enterprise, which fell on the victims of industrial accident. In one author's colourful metaphor, individuals blazed the trail but enterprises reaped the profits under the protection of the law (Green, 1953). We shall see that in this respect the pendulum has swung rather sharply: today, there is a counter tendency for judges to strain the fault concept in order to see "vulnerable victims" compensated by the imposition of liability on employers or corporate enterprise with "deep pockets".

The best way to describe the negligence principle, as it gradually established its predominance during the late nineteenth century, is as a set of mini-torts. The old common law imposed obligations in a number of disparate situations; a "bailee" entrusted with someone else's goods had to take good care of them; a "common carrier" owed a duty of care; dangerous chattels had to be looked after; and so on. But mere want of care was not in itself actionable; one of the common law duties needed to be shown. To quote from the contemporary case of *Heaven v Pender* (1883):

"Want of attention amounting to a want of ordinary care is not a good cause of action, although injury ensue from such a want unless the person charged with such want of ordinary care had a duty to the person complaining to use ordinary care in respect of the matter called in question."

The way in which the tort of negligence evolved, with duty as a prerequisite for liability, was once more to take the common law in a direction different to that taken in continental Europe. As the articles from the French Civil Code suggest, the focus of attention in systems based on Roman law is on the *fault*; instead, the common law focuses on the notion of *duty*, which serves as the primary regulator of liability in the tort of negligence (Stapleton, 1995b, pp.303–304). As common law duties crystallised into general principle, negligence acted as a catalyst, simplifying the common law and promoting change.

So persuaded were nineteenth-century authors of the justice of the fault principle that they began to view the remaining pockets of strict tortious liability as essentially unfair. Some legal historians (Winfield, 1926) went so far as to argue that "strict liability" or "liability without fault" had never existed; negligence was, they argued, implicit in the conduct of a person who let fire or cattle escape from his land or maintained a state of affairs amounting to a nuisance. Looking back, we can see that this analysis was incorrect (Gregory, 1951). Many examples can be given of strict liability in early law—such as liability for the escape of fire from one's property—where the strictness of the liability was expressed in the maxim that "a man must keep his fire in at his peril". Liability for "cattle trespass" arose when cattle escaped into neighbours" crops, and the escape of dangerous animals was another occasion for strict liability, a position anomalously maintained by s.4 of the Animals Act 1971. Even today, consolidation of tort law around the fault concept is not complete and, in later chapters, we shall come across further islands of strict liability left untouched by the principle of negligence established in *Donoghue v Stevenson*. Thus *nuisance*, a tort that developed at an early date to protect the occupier of land from damage or interference with his enjoyment of land attributable to a neighbouring landowner, was originally an area where the owner was strictly liable for damage occasioned by the nuisance. Fault was unnecessary. Later, we shall observe a fight to reduce this tort to an outlying branch of the law of negligence, as negligence, the general principle of liability, sweeps on (see below, p.84 *et seq*.).

Alongside the onward march of negligence, we find policymakers considering limited areas of a different and more modern type of strict liability. The Pearson Commission, set up in the wake of the thalidomide tragedy to advise on liability for personal injuries, favoured a "mixed system" of fault, "no fault" and strict liability for tort law (Pearson, 1978). Strict products liability took root in American law during the 1960s (Prosser, 1960, 1966), though recognised also in some continental systems. It reached the United Kingdom, where *Donoghue* still prevailed, after the European Commission, concerned with a "level playing field" for traders within the single market, issued a directive ordering the Member States to harmonise their laws on products liability. EC Directive 85/374 concerning liability for defective products was implemented in the United Kingdom by the Consumer Protection Act 1987. This Act introduced the strict liability principle in cases of physical injury caused by defective products circulated in the course of business, though subject to the "state of the art" defence in s.1(10). This section protects the producer from strict liability for products that reached recognised standards of safety at the time of manufacture, effectively reintroducing the notion of fault. Around the fringes of the Act and in cases of liability for services, negligence is still the law. The European Commission has also shown interest in strict liability for cases of environmental pollution in an effort to "make the polluter pay". These thoroughly confusing developments are outlined in Ch.5.

FROM PIGEONHOLE TO PRINCIPLE

Although negligence has gradually become the primary vehicle for changes to tort law, the old writ system is also occasionally capable of spawning new torts. In *Wilkinson v Downton* (1897), the defendant untruthfully told Mrs Wilkinson for a joke that her husband had been smashed up in an accident and that she was to go for him in a cab. The effect of this was to make her seriously ill from shock. On the face of it, this "wrong" was not actionable. The actions had been intentional, bringing the case into the ambit of trespass rather than negligence. But the "joke" did not amount to trespass to the person because no direct force was involved, so that it was not a battery; and no threat of force was involved, so that it was not an assault. Moreover, the damage suffered would today be called psychiatric injury or, in the language of the period, "nervous shock"; thus it was not the direct physical injury resulting from the use of force generally associated with trespass. Effectively, the judge was being asked to create an action that was not quite a trespass. In the legal terminology of the fourteenth century, he was being asked to allow an "action on the case". Precisely as his medieval forbears used to do when granting such an action, Wright J. awarded damages to Mrs Wilkinson.

By classifying nervous shock as physical injury, the judge made a significant innovation, which was to prove decidedly problematic in years to come (see below, p.68). More relevant to our argument at this stage, he also created a precedent in marginally stretching the framework of the tort of trespass to cover wilful wrongdoing that causes *indirect* physical harm. He also succeeded in reducing the elements of the tort that he was "creating" to a simple, general proposition that someone who wilfully does some act that causes injury is liable if the act does in fact cause harm:

"The defendant has . . . wilfully done an act calculated to cause physical harm to the female plaintiff, i.e., to infringe her right of personal safety, and has thereby in fact caused physical harm to her. This proposition, without more, appears to me to state a good cause of action, there being no justification alleged for the act."

Let us follow the way in which this precedent was to develop a little further. A few years later, private detectives called at a house and untruthfully told the maid that she was "wanted on suspicion of corresponding with a German spy". She too obtained damages for nervous shock (*Janvier v Sweeney*, 1919). In the course of his appellate judgement, Bankes L.J. said:

"Counsel for the defendant contended that no action would lie for words followed by such damage as the plaintiff alleges here. In order to sustain that contention it would be necessary to overrule

Wilkinson v Downton. In my opinion, that judgment was right. It has been approved in subsequent cases. It did not create any new rule of law, though it may be said to have extended existing principles over an area wider than that which they had been recognised as covering . . ."

Here we see a single precedent turning into a line of cases capable of moving the law of tort in several new directions.

Many years later, in *Khorasandjian v Bush* (1993), the two cases were considered in a rather different context. B had gone out with Miss K, who later wished to end the relationship. Not only did B abuse and assault her but he also followed up with a stream of telephone calls to her parents' house. A district judge awarded an injunction forbidding B from "harassing, pestering or communicating with" K in any way. B appealed on the ground that his language had not amounted to threats of force, therefore the facts did not reveal any tort known to the law and the conduct could not be restrained. Once again the court was being asked to extend the law because, in *Wilkinson* and *Janvier*, on which counsel relied heavily, there had been injury in the form of psychiatric illness; here, the telephone calls had not caused either fear or physical harm. Would the court once more extend the cause of action to create a tort of harassment without physical injury? The line of cases, which had already travelled far and fast, could usefully travel further (Conaghan, 1993; Bridgeman and Jones, 1994).

Perhaps unfortunately, an alternative way to provide redress existed. The law of nuisance, which protects the owner or occupier of land from interference with his use or enjoyment of the land, could be extended. The extension was necessary because Miss K lived with her parents and was not the home-owner. Marginal extension of the law of nuisance to cover family members was the option preferred by the Court of Appeal. As so often happens, therefore, the law shortly afterwards took a step backward. *Hunter v Canary Wharf* (1997; see below, p.86) brought the promising line of cases to an abrupt end. The House of Lords ruled that the right to sue in private nuisance had always been restricted to the owner or occupier and to extend the right would create anomalies. Criticising the reasoning of the Court of Appeal in *Khorasandjian*, Lord Goff identified the "gist of the tort" as *harassment* rather than *nuisance*. The telephone calls were not restricted to the home but could follow Miss K from place to place, reaching her mobile telephone as she walked. The law of private nuisance should not be exploited in order to "create by the back door a tort of harassment which was only partly effective in that it was artificially limited to harassment which takes place in her home". In *Wainwright v Home Office* (2003), the House of Lords closed the door more firmly. Here damages were sought for an unauthorised strip search, which again fell outside the tort of trespass because no touching was involved; the claimant, Mrs Wainwright, had been told to undress and had, unwillingly, complied. Later she brought an action on the ground that the prison officers had not complied with the relevant prison rules. On appeal to the House of Lords, Lord Hoffmann asserted that *Wilkinson* did not provide a remedy for distress falling short of "recognized psychiatric injury", casting doubt on the validity of that bold precedent by adding, "so far as there may be a tort of intention under which such damage is recoverable, the necessary intention was not established".

If we return to Street's analysis of tort law, we can see that the judges have by and large been anxious to protect the various claimants against malicious and intentional types of conduct that have caused damage. The problem has been with Street's first question: What interests does the law of torts protect? Behind most of these cases we can sense a more abstract idea of intrusion into someone's autonomous private space. As we shall see in Ch.7, however, no right to privacy is as yet recognised by English law. This omission leaves English judges to scratch around in the law of torts to find a way to protect privacy, falling back on the antiquated forms of action and methodology of the law of torts. The approach of Lord Bingham, a specialist in the subject, when asked to consider in an academic article how English judges might respond to claims of damages for violations of human rights, is very significant. Lord Bingham's approach was first to list interests in the nature of privacy protected by tort law and then to run through the existing cases to estimate how far it was in fact protected (Bingham, 1998): what we might term the index approach to tort law. "We have buried the forms of action but they still rule us from their graves."

COURTS, PARLIAMENT AND TORT LAW

The tort law that we have today is a much-patched garment. The body is made of the tort of negligence. The sleeves and pockets are still the nominate torts, some more important than others. The patches are sometimes put on by Parliament and sometimes by the judges. But tort law is not a great vote winner and Parliament tends to leave to judges what judges would prefer to leave to Parliament. Government may intervene when some specific problem is drawn to its attention, especially if—as was the case with the legislation covering guard dogs—some hideous accident has caught the imagination of the public and created a temporary "vote winner". Rather differently, the Lord Chancellor's Department (now the Department of Constitutional Affairs) sometimes acts with a consolidating or unexciting departmental "miscellaneous provisions" measure that brings together a number of odds and ends, such as the Administration of Justice Act 1982, which groups some important changes to the law of damages with other, very different provisions. Much-needed reform may have to await the chance of a Private Member emulating Lord Campbell, as with the Dangerous Dogs Act 1989. Today, however, the slots for Private Members' Bills are strictly limited, with parliamentary time controlled by government. The Law Commission, set up specifically to bring problems of "lawyers' law" to public notice, has not to date undertaken a general tort law programme or, indeed, yet completed its project for codification of the law of contract. Its first general project in the area of tort law has been a wide-ranging review of the law of damages (Law Com.1997a, 1998, 1999), one of tort law's most problematic areas. This is now complete but it still awaits action. Codification is once again on the back burner.

A further example of the dysfunctional relationship between the bodies responsible for tort law is what occurred in reforming the common law concerning liability of property owners (or occupiers) for accidents taking place on their land and premises. The common law rules were complex, unsatisfactory and unfair, giving rise to much litigation and many "hard cases". A Law Reform Committee set up specifically to examine the problem urged that action should be taken to clarify the law. For once Parliament accepted the recommendation and provided a codification in the Occupiers' Liability Act 1957 of liability to "lawful visitors". This term applies to everyone who comes on to property with the permission, explicit or implicit, of the property owner or occupier. But typically, the codification was incomplete. It left unresolved the most controversial issue: liability to trespassers, who come on to property without the owner's consent.

The attitude of the common law to trespassers was severe and even occasionally barbaric; the use of mantraps to deter poachers was originally sanctioned. The duty owed by landowners has always been the low one of not deliberately or wilfully causing them injury. But trespassers range from burglars injured in the course of their unlawful and unpopular activities to small children, who are classic "vulnerable victims". They may wander on to unprotected premises or be attracted on to them by a state of affairs that offers a good opportunity to play (as in the case of *Hughes v Lord Advocate* (1963, see below p.66), where a tent and a lantern provided the occasion for a tragic accident). The common law had dealt differently with different categories of trespasser and, some years after the 1957 Act, the House of Lords stepped in to moderate and generalise the harsh rules. In *Herrington v British Railways Board* (1972), a small child had wandered on to a railway track through a hole in the fence. The House held the Board liable, imposing a "duty of common humanity" to trespassers. Once again the law was in a state of confusion. No one knew precisely what a duty of common humanity was and how it differed on one side from a duty of care and on the other from a duty not recklessly to cause injury. So the landmark decision was referred to the Law Commission for consideration (Cmnd.6428, 1976). This report was not implemented until Lord Hailsham, then Lord Chancellor, a Cabinet minister in search of a legislative project, finally dusted it down and sent it to Parliament to pass the Occupiers' Liability Act 1984. Once again, this Act is complex and difficult to interpret and, unlike the Scottish legislation, it does not consolidate the law by picking up the 1957 Act and covering both lawful visitors and trespassers, leaving some notably hard cases for the judges. (For the case law, see Hepple, Howarth and Matthews, 2000, pp.578–583). Even this is not the end of the story: in the year 2000, modifications were made to occupiers' liability by s.13 of the Countryside and Rights of Way Act. None of this disparate legislation is codified.

As the attitude of Parliament to the courts in the area of tort law is, generally speaking, one of laissez-faire, the courts might very well deduce from parliamentary inertia that they were being given carte blanche to develop the common law as they thought fit, as they in fact did in *Herrington*. But the constitutional position as understood by a majority of the judiciary does not seem to permit this. Once judges depart too far from the traditional path of precedent, they are afraid to be seen as stepping outside their constitutional role by indulging in policymaking and they may hesitate to step across the invisible boundary between deciding cases and making new law. Invisible boundaries are, of course, problematic as they vary on different occasions according to the opinions of different judges. Why, for example, did the bold decision in *Wilkinson* not cross the boundary, when *Khorasandjian* apparently did?

The dilemma was summarised by Lord Scarman in yet another hard case concerning nervous shock (*McLoughlin v O'Brian*, 1982). A father and his three children were gravely injured in a traffic accident. The mother, who was not with them, very naturally went to see her family in hospital and the sight of their sufferings produced such serious trauma that she became ill from depression. Would the House of Lords allow liability to be extended to someone not actually in physical danger or even present at the accident? Here Lord Scarman advocates a positive approach:

"The appeal raises directly a question as to the balance in our law between the functions of judge and legislature. The common law covers everything that is not covered by statute. It knows no gaps . . . The function of the court is to decide the case before it, even though the decision may require the extension or adaptation of a principle or in some cases the creation of new law to meet the justice of the case. But whatever the court decides to do, it starts from a baseline of existing principle and seeks a solution consistent with or analogous to a principle or principles already recognised.

The distinguishing feature of the common law is this judicial development and formulation of principle. Policy considerations will have to be weighed; but the objective of the judges is the formulation of principle. And if principle inexorably requires a decision which entails a degree of policy risk, the court's function is to adjudicate according to principle, leaving policy curtailment to the judgment of Parliament . . . If principle leads to results which are thought to be socially unacceptable, Parliament can legislate to draw a line or map out a new path."

But in another hard case Lord Pearson advised a more cautious line. The "family car" was driven with the permission of the husband, when the wife was the person technically insured. In the light of their knowledge that third party insurance for traffic accidents was compulsory, the Court of Appeal held the wife vicariously liable for the driver's negligence in causing an accident, reasoning that the car was being used by a member of the family and it would be unreasonable if, in this type of situation, the family were to find themselves uninsured (*Morgans v Launchbury*, 1973). This doctrine of the "family car", however worthy, was entirely novel and involved a considerable extension of the law. The House of Lords thought that the wife was *not* liable and this is what, Lord Pearson, at the time chairing a Royal Commission on Civil Liability for Personal Injuries (Pearson, 1978), had to say:

"It seems to me that these innovations, whether or not they may be desirable, are not suitable to be introduced by judicial decision. They raise difficult questions of policy, as well as involving the introduction of new legal principles rather than extension of some principle already recognized and operating. The questions of policy need consideration by the government and Parliament, using the sources at their command for making wide enquiries and gathering evidence and opinions as to the practical effects of the proposed innovations. Apart from the transitional difficulty of current policies of insurance being rendered insufficient by judicial changes in the law, there is the danger of injustice to owners who for one reason or another are not adequately covered by insurance or perhaps not effectively insured at all (e. g. if they have forgotten to renew their policies or have taken out policies which are believed by them to be valid but are in fact invalid, or have taken their policies from an insolvent insurance company). Moreover, lack of insurance cover would in some cases defeat the object of the proposed innovation, because uninsured or insufficiently insured owners would often be unable to pay damages, awarded against them in favour of injured plaintiffs. Any extension of car owners' liability ought to be accompanied by an extension of effective insurance cover. How would that be brought about? And how would it be paid for? Would the owner of the car be required to take out a policy for the benefit of any person who may drive a car? Would there be an exception for some kinds of unlawful driving? A substantial increase in premiums for motor insurance would be likely to result and to have an inflationary effect on costs and prices. It seems to me that if the proposed innovations are desirable, they should be introduced not by judicial decision but by legislation after suitable investigation and full consideration of the questions of policy involved."

Would Lord Pearson have decided the same way, if he had known that, 15 years after this judgment was delivered, and nearly 10 years after the Pearson Commission finally reported, Parliament would have done absolutely nothing? We are still without a doctrine of the "family car" and for that matter, without any other far-reaching reform of tort law. The House of Lords might have speeded a necessary reform by deciding in favour of the "family car" doctrine and leaving it to Parliament, no doubt at the invitation of the powerful insurance lobby, to excise the doctrine from the law if it wished to do so. That is indeed how the

Court of Appeal responded, many years later, to another demand for reform. In *Heil v Rankin* (2000), a special, five-man Court of Appeal was summoned to hear eight selected cases dealing with the level of damages for pain and suffering in personal injuries litigation. The Court was acting primarily on a Law Commission report on personal injuries damages, recently presented to the Lord Chancellor but not yet implemented by Parliament (Law Com.257, 1999). Before moving to uprate damages, as the report recommended, the Court of Appeal invited representations from some of those likely to be affected, amongst them insurers, the ambulance service and health authorities (a rather random choice of advisers). The Court then decided to adopt the Law Commission's main recommendations, though not all of them. The judges had not, of course, *legislated*. The way was still left open for Parliament to do so and perhaps if the powerful insurance lobby or National Health Service had made enough fuss Parliament would have excised *Heil* from the law. What the Court of Appeal did nonetheless remains a questionable procedure in a parliamentary democracy, and one that leaves the judiciary wide open to charges of judicial lawmaking.

TORT LAW AND INSURANCE

Morgans v Launchbury, where the judges talked openly of insurance, was in one respect a quite exceptional case. It is significant because it draws our attention to tort law's best-kept secret: that in practice, the cost of almost all tort actions is met by insurance. In this introductory book we shall look at a large number of cases, in some of which we shall find that very high sums in damages have been awarded. Damages in the medical negligence cases discussed in Ch.4 may, for example, reach many thousands of pounds. Very occasionally, a hint is found in judgments that insurance has a part to play in meeting the costs.

Throughout the nineteenth century, when fault held sway and the elements of punishment and deterrence in tort law were not closely questioned, the sale of liability insurance was considered to be contrary to public policy (Davies, 1989). Today, everything has changed. Employers, responsible under the doctrine of vicarious liability for accidents at work caused to and by their employees and increasingly targeted in workplace accidents, have by law to purchase a measure of third-party insurance against liability for death and personal injury. Sometimes third-party insurance is compulsory, as it is in many circumstances for motorists; without compulsory road traffic insurance, the average driver would certainly not be able to meet the costs even of minor accidents. Manufacturers insure against liability for loss caused by defects in their products. Individuals also need insurance. Owners and occupiers of property need to be insured against liability for damage caused by the defective state of premises and their liability too is being extended, sometimes in ways that make insurance difficult. Household policies often cover liability for accidents caused by the householder, sometimes even outside the home or property. Other losses may be covered by first party insurance; relatives of a murder victim may recover under a life policy or a householder may insure against theft. Doctors, nurses and health authorities are all insured against professional negligence and many professionals—lawyers, accountants and surveyors—are insured against the risks of their profession. Other professions are increasingly being sucked into the insurance net as liability extends to teachers, police and social workers. Local authorities, nationalised industries and other public bodies are very heavily insured, though central government continues to carry its own risks. We are talking about huge sums of money. An enormous industry has grown up around tort law, with judges indirectly acting as insurance agents. Without the insurance industry, tort law quite simply would not survive!

Yet we do not know how many of the tort actions described here were in fact fought and defended purely by insurers, because nominally they are fought by and in the name of individuals. In *Stovin v Wise*, a road accident case (see below, p.146), Lord Nicholls tacitly admitted that the case was really about insurance and asked whether anything of social utility was to be gained by shifting the financial loss from the insurers of road users to those of a local authority? But the House of Lords did not directly address the insurance position, arguably central to the outcome, nor does the case tell us who the real claimant was and whether all or only some of the parties were insured. Were the insurers perhaps seeking to establish liability in order that an apportionment could be made?

Again, in a recent case where the Court of Appeal was considering whether or not to impose liability on the referee of a rugby football match for an accident suffered by one of the players, insurance clearly lay behind the decision. We know this because the trial judge remarked in the course of his judgment that, when rugby was well funded by gate receipts plus "lucrative television contracts", there was no reason why the union should not insure its referees: "amateur rugby players will be young men mostly with very limited income. Insurance cover for referees would be a cost spread across the whole game." This was pure speculation on which no evidence had been heard and which was in fact inaccurate. Yet when the remarks were contested at the appeal hearing, all that the Court would say was that the judge's assumptions were "reasonable" (*Vowles v Evans*, 2003, p.1614).

The argument for excluding evidence about insurance is based on the traditional view of tort law as a relationship between two individuals. If this bipolar relationship is undercut by consideration of insurance then, so the argument runs, tort law will lose its internal coherence and ultimately its very reason for existence (Stapleton, 1995a). The case for bringing the insurance position into the open is, however, much stronger. To allocate a loss to an individual, such as a householder or small landowner, who is uninsured and unable to obtain insurance, is ineffective and arguably unfair. Lack of transparency about the true actors lends an added air of unreality to tort law.

CONCLUSION

The picture of tort law that we are beginning to assemble is of a collection of disparate torts and interests protected by the common law. We are not yet in a position to put names to all of the torts that the common law recognises, though we have met a handful: trespass, nuisance and negligence are already on our list. Understanding tort law would be so much easier if we could only pin it down!

Although we do not yet know precisely which interests are protected, we know that physical integrity comes high on the list. We have looked at some of the ways in which the common law can be updated, as it was when judges bent the trespass frame to accommodate a claimant who had suffered injury from a deliberate wrongful act. The most significant evolution took place in the late nineteenth and early twentieth centuries, when negligence evolved. We shall look more closely at the rise of negligence in Ch.3. Tort law, we have learned, is one of the main ways to obtain compensation for personal injury. Finally, we saw that many of tort law's most frustrating characteristics derive from the unsatisfactory relationship between courts and Parliament. Tort law has not been codified or systematically reformed. A pattern has developed of short, specific measures aimed at replacing common law rules that have shown themselves to be unsatisfactory or filling gaps in the common law. The interplay between courts and legislature has turned tort law into something of a patchwork, with legislative patches roughly tacked on to the fabric of the common law.

The common law of torts originated in a rural society, where centralised justice was just being born. It has lasted through an industrial revolution to play a major part in compensating the victims of industrial and transport accidents. It now has to cope with a centralised and highly regulated state, in which a "compensation culture" is starting to emerge. The victim-oriented ethos thrown up by our consumer society has contributed largely to the rapid expansion of modern tort law (White, 1980, p.xv; Schwartz, 1992; Sugarman, 2000). The compensation culture makes the assumption that "vulnerable victims" are almost automatically entitled to compensation when events do not go their way; someone else must be to blame for their injuries. We are moving into a period when security from untoward happenings is beginning to seem a fundamental human right. How the courts meet these new and intriguing challenges and whether tort law is capable of an adequate response, we shall see in the following chapters.

FURTHER READING

The best historical survey of the emergence of negligence as a discrete tort is still Winfield, "Duty in Tortious Negligence" (1934) 34 *Columbia Law Review* 41. See also Gregory, "Trespass to Negligence to Absolute Liability" (1951) 37 *Virginia Law Review* 359. Harlow, "A Treatise For Our Times?" (1984) 47 *Modern Law Review* 487 gives a short introduction to the development of tort texts. Sugarman's article, "A Century of Change in Personal Injuries Law" (2000) 88 *California Law Review* 2403 leads nicely through to coming chapters. Cane's *Anatomy of Tort Law* (Oxford, Hart Publishing, 1997) is an ambitious attempt at a coherent and logical classification that restructures and casts new light on the antiquated "law of torts". Finally, no one interested in legal history can fail to enjoy White, *Tort Law in America, An Intellectual History* (Oxford, Oxford University Press, 1980).

2

THE AIMS OF TORT LAW

TORT LAW AND CORRECTIVE JUSTICE

The approach of lawyers and judges in common law systems is not especially academic nor do they usually take much interest in deep theory. By and large, amongst lawyers, pragmatism is the order of the day (Atiyah, 1987b). In this respect, the approach taken so far in this book has been highly traditional. Chapter 1 treated tort law as a journey through time, its present shape and imperfections dictated largely by its history. True, we looked briefly at some theoretical attempts to classify tort law but these were efforts to produce a coherent theoretical framework, explanatory mapping carried out within the parameters of the existing law. This chapter moves away from Street's definition of tort law (1983, p.3) as a "regime of correlative rights and duties" concerned with "those situations where the conduct of one party causes or threatens harm to the interests of other parties", to examine tort law's wider objectives.

Attempting to distinguish tort from crime, we described tort as a vehicle for compensation, a view widely shared by modern judges, amongst whom considerable continuity is in fact found. Sir Anthony Mason, previously Chief Justice of Australia, recently described tort law as designed to adjust "losses and afford compensation for injuries sustained as a result of the conduct of another". His proposition was borrowed from a leading academic half a century before (Mason, 1998, p.13; Wright, 1942, p.238). In line with the same individualistic view of tort law, Lord Bingham recently described its overall objective as "to define cases in which the law may justly hold one party liable to compensate another" (*Fairchild v Glenhaven Funeral Services*, 2002).

Amongst legal theorists and philosophers, this individualist analysis is known as the "corrective justice" model of tort law (Weinrib, 1989). This term denotes "a system of rights and duties that are correlative between identified persons and stem solely from a particular event" (Morris, 1995, p.205)—precisely what we have so far been describing. But this currently fashionable philosophical justification for tort law in fact encompasses several contrary conceptions. Some corrective justice theories stress the victim's loss, taking the elimination or annulment of so-called wrongful losses to be the point of corrective justice: in other words, a victim-oriented theory. Other theorists start from the defendant's conduct: it is because the defendant has acted wrongfully towards the defendant that the victim has a right to be compensated; such a theory might, as argued in the previous chapter, be more favourable to the defendant (Perry, 1993, p.24). Equally, taking the defendant's wrongdoing as a starting point might encourage an emphasis on tort law's deterrent functions.

Both in historical formulations of tort law and in corrective justice theories, the "rightness" of fault liability is made to seem permanent and unchallengeable—deliberately so. André Tunc speaks of the "slow, uncertain but on the whole majestic emergence of the principle that a man is liable for the damage caused by his fault" (Tunc, 1972, p.249), an evolution that we traced broadly to the nineteenth century, though one to which earlier generations had substantially contributed. The fault principle's enduring strength derives from religious and cultural connections—the biblical origins of Lord Atkin's "neighbour" test in *Donoghue* (see below, p.48) are self-evident. For a less religious age, Sir Arthur Goodhart recast tort law's ethical dimension, remarking that a moral law based on reason rather than religion "seems to be the one which has most influence in English law". Goodhart went on to link Lord Atkin's "good neighbour" metaphor with his own personal belief in rationality as the basis for the common law; it represents a basic morality "necessary for the good life both of the individual and the community" (Goodhart, 1953, p.37). This is the pragmatic or "commonsense" view of the law, linked to community morality through the ideas of "reasonableness" and "neighbourliness" and summed up in the seductive and misleading image of "the reasonable man", who acts as the standard of care expected in the tort of negligence. What the "man on the Clapham omnibus" really thinks of tort law we cannot know, other than that the public is naturally susceptible to stories of "hard cases", fanned by the media. We may today want to note the growth of a "compensation culture", which provides a financial motive to seek out someone who can be blamed for accidents and, in parallel, of a "blame culture", in which tort law acts as machinery for accountability as well as for compensation. A "popular sense of justice" is, however, almost impossible to identify.

A CRITIQUE OF TORT LAW

To radical and critical legal theorists, the orthodox presentation of tort law as apolitical and justifiable in terms of a shared community morality is itself a highly political position. Like all law, they would argue, tort law reflects the values over time of a capitalist and individualist society. In the carefully neutral evaluations of the classic corrective justice theory, or the "black-letter" textbooks to which students turn to find "the law", lie buried a set of assumptions unacceptable to radical lawyers and critical legal theorists. They do not wish to reduce tort law to a set of coherent principles or to judge it by its logical coherence or even by its effectiveness as a system of accident compensation; instead, they emphasise its arbitrary outcomes and the "underlying callousness of its ideology" (Conaghan and Mansell, 1993). Even if such authors by and large disapprove the underlying assumptions of modern tort law, they are more concerned to point out that these embody value judgments of a kind normally labelled "political". They want an alternative, political history of tort law to be written.

Radical lawyers protest about the limitations on the protected interests of tort law, reproaching it for its inadequacies and omissions. They point to whole classes of person excluded, or virtually excluded, from its protection. Feminists argue that tort law reflects male standards of reasonableness and protects interests valued by males rather than females. They campaign for an extension of tort law to provide protection against sexual harassment and abuse, as it notably failed to do after *Khorasandjian* (Conaghan, 1998). They cite the case of rape, a traumatic injury often with long-term psychological effects. But in *Meah v McCreamer* (1985, 1986), M, a passenger in the car of a drunken driver, suffered head injuries, resulting in severe brain damage. He went on to commit a number of sexual offences, including a rape, which earned him a life sentence. Arguing that this was the outcome of a personality change caused by the head injuries, M included in his claim for damages from the driver his "loss of amenity" and was awarded £60,000 in damages. Not unnaturally, the victims, who had respectively received compensation of £1,000 for sexual assault and £3,000 for rape from the Criminal Injuries Compensation Scheme, felt somewhat aggrieved when they read in the newspapers of this award; consulting lawyers, they duly brought an action against M. The same judge awarded them £6,750 for the sexual assault and £10,250 for the rape (*W and D v Meah*, 1986).

Critical theorists focus on injustice to individuals or groups of individuals. A more general critique is that, if tort law did not lure us into acceptance of its limited compensatory purpose—that *individual* victims of wrongdoing must be restored to their previous financial position by any wrongdoer found to be at fault— then we might turn our ingenuity to producing a more caring society, in which all incapacity was treated more sympathetically. Far from tort law being the "last outpost of the welfare state", as recently labelled by an Australian judge (Spigelman, 2002), there would be no further need for tort law (Abel, 1982).

LOSS SPREADING AND ENTERPRISE LIABILITY

In Ch.1, it was suggested that Oliver Wendell Holmes, arguing for fault liability, was expressing a fairly general nineteenth-century preference, based on contemporary political and economic beliefs. In a strikingly modern passage from *The Common Law*, Holmes had this to say about possible bases for tort liability:

"The state might conceivably make itself a mutual insurance company against accidents, and distribute the burden of its citizens' mishaps among all its members. There might be a pension for paralytics, and state aid for those who suffered in person or estate from tempest or wild beasts . . . or it might throw all loss upon the actor irrespective of fault. The state does none of these things, however, and the prevailing view is that its cumbrous and expensive machinery ought not to be set in motion unless some clear benefit is to be derived from disturbing the *status quo*. State interference is an evil, when it cannot be shown to be a good. Universal insurance, if desired, can be better and more cheaply accomplished by private enterprise. The undertaking to redistribute losses simply on the ground that they resulted from the defendant's act would not only be open to these objections, but . . . to the still greater one of offending the sense of justice. Unless my act is of a nature to threaten others, unless under the circumstances a prudent man would have foreseen the possibility of harm, it is no more justifiable to make me indemnify my neighbor against the consequences, than to make me do the same thing if I had fallen upon him in a fit, or to compel me to insure him against lightning." (Holmes, 1906, pp.77–78)

With hindsight, we can see that this robust defence of fault liability is, as the critical legal theorist would certainly argue, riddled with value judgments. The use of the term "state interference" creates a presumption that state intervention is an evil. It creates a presumption against collective action, an antipathy mirrored in the opening remarks. These are dismissive of state pensions "for paralytics" and of state insurance for accidents. What did Holmes think of workmen's compensation legislation, at the time he wrote fairly new on the scene? The worldwide move towards workers' compensation legislation in the last decade of the nineteenth century suggests that the elected representatives of the people did not in general see compensation for injured workers as unjust. It was leaving the cost of accidents to fall on individual victims badly placed to insure against risk that seemed unjust. But perhaps this is a specifically American viewpoint, linked to a robust American individualism? Not all of Holmes's American contemporaries would have accepted his dogmatic assertions as axiomatic. A contemporary article in the *Harvard Law Review* (Ballantine, 1916) advocates a scheme of state compensation in the case of railway accidents as sophisticated as any of the modern schemes discussed in later chapters. Holmes's views are in short contestable; it is not the case, for example, that compensation without fault necessarily "offends the sense of justice"; some authors prefer strict liability and, in selected areas, strict liability is today the favourite with legislators. Time has made other statements controvertible. Empirical evidence for the superiority of private over public insurance is not by and large on Holmes's side (Corfield, 1984).

If the paramount concern of the nineteenth-century scholar was the construction of a principled system of tort law, rational and coherent in its own terms, then the dominant twentieth-century ideology was a preoccupation with rationality and efficiency. During that century, tort law's efficiency as a vehicle for accident compensation came under rigorous scrutiny. Shortly after the Second World War, Friedmann was arguing that tort law's main function was "the reasonable adjustment of economic risks . . . and not the expression of certain absolute moral principles" (Friedmann, 1949). Concern with the *ineffectiveness* of the tort system in shifting the cost of accidents is only one dimension of Patrick Atiyah's seminal book, *Accidents, Compensation and the Law,* first published in 1970. Underlying the study also is an idealistic concern with the *inequalities* of tort law. As seen by Atiyah, tort law is not merely a "forensic lottery" (Ison, 1967); tort law mirrors the capitalist system in singling out some claimants for comparative riches, while others in similar cases are not permitted to recover. A rational and compassionate society, Atiyah argues, ought not to tolerate arbitrary divisions between the sick and disabled; between disability due to injury and disability due to disease; between physical and psychological illness; between the victims of criminal violence and of road accidents. Society ought to treat everyone "with common humanity". Atiyah is describing a substitute for tort law and one based on very different premises to the individualist notions so far encountered. He suggests a compensation system based on the idea of "social insurance", directly comparable to and perhaps part of the social security system. Currently fashionable philosophical theories of "corrective justice" would treat this functionalist objective as falling outside the proper domain of tort law, which they see as the bipolar, private law regime of correlative rights and duties (Weinrib, 1995, p.19). But Atiyah's contribution was to move the topic of accident compensation in a period of socialist politics out of the corrective justice paradigm of tort law and towards a "distributive justice" model, in which there would be a fairer and more equal "sharing of the cake" and distribution of resources.

Tort law, the corrective justice theorist would retort, is not about equality; this is the field of distributive justice. Yet in modern times, it has to be admitted that tort law has assumed a substantial "loss shifting" function. Some of the theories that seek to shift losses from the victim to those best able to pay are cynically described as "deep pocket" theories of tort law; they operate by pushing liability on to the shoulders of large corporate or public bodies best able to absorb or spread the losses. Traditionally, this has been done through development of the twin ideas of vicarious liability, which makes an employer liable for the acts of his employees; and of employers' liability, which imposes a duty of care on employers to render the workplace reasonably safe (*Wilsons and Clyde Coal Co v English*, 1938). These doctrines are seen by some as an offshoot of managerial reform in the late nineteenth century, when workmen's compensation schemes and compulsory insurance were first introduced (Witt, 2003). It is generally agreed that tort law's period of great expansion runs from the 1960s to the 1980s, when judges in the common law countries were at their most creative. Gary Schwartz (1992) has labelled the American victim-oriented case law of this period a collection of "plaintiff's greatest hits". Peter Huber (1988, p.4) describes it as a "tort tax". Since then, Schwartz thinks that judges have become more cautious; they have "rejected invitations to endorse new innovations in liability; moreover they have placed a somewhat conservative gloss on innovations undertaken in previous years".

But amongst litigants, the search for deeper and deeper pockets moved on. We started with a concept of employers' liability that was "vicarious" or secondary in character. We moved with the introduction of the non-delegable duty of care to impose liability on the employer "as the primary actor" (McKendrick, 1990). This enabled a further extension of the technical devices used for loss shifting, to take in other peripheral parties (Stapleton, 1995b). Modern litigants and their lawyers seek to shift losses on to public services and public authorities, whose treasuries are seen as inexhaustible. The retreat of the 1980s towards what came to be called "incrementalism" represented a changed and more conservative economic and political climate. The rise of the "regulatory state", which encourages competition and private enterprise while at the same time regulating its activities, has created new spheres of operation for tort lawyers (see Ch.8). This trend back to liability is currently being stimulated by the growth of human rights litigation (see Ch.7).

Atiyah's pessimistic conclusion was that, even in its most expansive period, tort law could not satisfactorily carry out a loss spreading function and that it should be replaced with a true social insurance plan, funded by the taxpayer. By no means every legal theorist would accept this collectivist conclusion. In the same expansive period of tort law, economic theorists differently placed on the political spectrum also focused on tort law's efficiency as a vehicle for accident compensation. Rooted in microeconomics, this type of risk or loss-spreading theory is more optimistic about tort law's rational potential, which is seen as a free market mechanism for "risk allocation". These theorists proffer economic analyses of tort law, based on the paradigm of the market and of "rational man", a businessman or manufacturer concerned to find the cheapest way to operate within a market economy, inviting the reader to choose between competing economic models. Belief in tort law as a deterrent, which will persuade "rational, economic man" to cut his costs by accident prevention, is central to many of these economic theories.

Green (1953, p.775) saw enterprise liability as a suitable vehicle for "a more comprehensive and more adequate means of protection for all victims of personal injuries ... without placing too heavy a burden on enterprise or any other segment of the social group". Guido Calabresi (1961), in his celebrated theory of enterprise liability, advocated that "activities should bear the costs they engender"; the liability of manufacturers is, for example, justifiable because they are well placed to pass on the cost to their consumers, who benefit from the product. There is, however, little agreement as to how losses can best be allocated (Priest, 1985). Should they be passed on directly to consumers, redistributed through insurance or allocated to the general public through the tax system? The answer chosen may depend not only on political standpoint but also whether compensation or deterrence is chosen as tort law's primary goal. There is further disagreement about the *standard* of liability to be selected. There is little consensus amongst theorists as to what might be substituted for the present principles of negligence liability. Calabresi (1970) and Brian Epstein (1973) both favoured strict liability as a more efficient tool for transferring an insurable risk to defendants. Strict liability also contains a stronger element of deterrence. Provided no fault-based defences are introduced as a torpedo, the clear and simple message of the early nominate torts, "Do this at your peril!" is replicated in the message of modern strict liability. Yet Richard Posner (1973), an ardent exponent of free market economic theory, prefers the traditional negligence doctrine as the optimal standard for liability, because it combines a sense of justice with efficiency, "Take care or pay up!" Only the costs of their own negligence are allocated to the parties at fault, allowing them to calculate the costs of non-compliance more precisely.

To translate these economic models into the principles and terminology of tort law is not particularly easy. There is, however, one celebrated attempt to do so within the law of negligence. In *United States v Carroll Towing Co* (1947), an American court had to decide whether a barge owner owed a duty of care to keep a watchman on board when the barge was in harbour. According to Judge Learned Hand, the court must weigh the following three variables:

- the probability that the barge would break away;
- the gravity of the resulting injury, if it did;
- the burden of adequate precautions.

This process he expressed in terms of the following equation, usually known as "the Learned Hand formula":

"If the probability be called P; the injury, L; and the burden, B; liability depends upon whether B is less than L multiplied by P: i.e., whether B [is less than] PL."

As Epstein (1973, p.154) shrewdly remarks, after this one algebraic effort, the Learned Hand judgment contains "a marked shift in the style and logic of opinion, which suggests that after all [the judge] is more concerned with the traditional questions of 'reasonableness' than with the systematic application of his economic formula". We might deduce that, if courts are to operate as the main vehicle for the covert introduction of enterprise liability, they will only be comfortable in so doing if they can move in this direction without abandoning the familiar terminology of tort law. Indeed, Ch.1 has told us that the doctrine of precedent, at least as it operates in the United Kingdom, actually dictates this solution in the absence of any substantial guidance from the legislature. Judges who move overtly into the business of developing tort law as a loss-spreading system step outside their constitutional territory on to the terrain of Parliament and, by so doing, imperil the apolitical reputation of tort law.

Even in the United Kingdom, where the judiciary is traditionally circumspect over policy-making functions, steps in the direction of enterprise liability are still possible. In addition to the concepts of vicarious liability and non-delegable duty, the idea of "breach of statutory duty" has been invoked to impose strict liability in specific cases, while preserving the negligence action as the *general* standard of liability. In *John Summers v Frost* (1955), a worker's thumb was amputated by a grindstone, dangerous machinery that by statute had to be "securely fenced". The employers' defence was that the machinery had been fenced as securely as was humanly possible; any further guard would have rendered the machine unusable. The employers were nonetheless held liable. Analysed in terms of the prevailing orthodoxy of fault-based liability, this decision warrants the label of "affront to commonsense" bestowed on it by Professor Glanville Williams (1960, p.238). It must be unjust to hold the careful employer liable for something which due care cannot prevent. A theory of enterprise liability would, on the other hand, justify the judgment on grounds of expediency; if a given risk cannot entirely be prevented, then it should fall on the enterprise which creates it and which makes the profit. The loss can be easily spread, either by including it as a manufacturing cost or through insurance, which the manufacturer/employer is best placed to secure.

But even in this field of industrial accidents, where enterprise liability is most appropriate and easiest to procure, the fault concept is always creeping back. In *Davie v New Merton Board Mills* (1959), a worker was blinded when a chip from the tool he was using sheered off and flew into his eye; outwardly perfect, the tool actually concealed a dangerous manufacturing flaw. The worker was apparently on strong ground in suing his employer, as the case seemed to fall squarely within the concept of employers' non-delegable duty of care. To the surprise of many, the House of Lords held the duty discharged because the tool had been purchased from a reputable supplier; thus the loss fell on the worker, unlikely to have been insured and probably unable also to prove fault by the supplier and manufacturer. Whatever its justification in terms of fault, this outcome is indefensible in terms of enterprise liability. It creates confusion, inciting insurers to litigate over who is to pay for a risk when both have accepted premiums; it leaves the victim with alternative remedies in tort and contract against different defendants, both of whom may be able to prove that they were not liable; and, at the end of the day, it leaves the loss to fall on the worker, the one person in the triangle who is least likely to be insured or to be able to find competitive rates of insurance. The predictable response to this decision from government was "law reform by penny numbers"; in a typically limited exercise, the decision was wiped out by the Employer's Liability (Defective Equipment) Act 1969.

In the area of employers' liability, the competing ideologies of fault and loss shifting through enterprise liability have contributed to a complex body of law that no one can properly explain or understand. During the early years of the century, in an attempt to do justice to workers, courts allowed negligence liability to be buttressed by the action based on breach of statutory duty. But these duties had to be picked out from general legislation and a 'haphazard mass of ill-assorted regulations', which dealt separately with different industries: mining and quarries regulations, regulations governing the use of explosives or of dangerous pollutants, and so on. Some of these were framed in terms of negligence, specifying that employers should take such care as was reasonable or practicable; others imposed strict liability; while a majority failed entirely to state whether or not civil liability was intended. In an attempt to tidy up the situation, the Health and Safety at Work Act 1974 introduced a general standard of liability based, after much argument, on negligence. It goes without saying that no thorough attempt at codification has ever been made. What is left is an incoherent network of inherently contradictory provisions, which have to be adjusted by courts to the incompatible objectives of compensation, prevention and deterrence, which are all legitimate goals for such legislation.

RATIONAL MAN AND DETERRENCE

Economic theories of tort law place a heavy emphasis on deterrence, stressing the extent to which fear of tort damages can spur businesses to minimise the cost of accidents by taking precautions. The theories envisage a notional balancing process in which the cost of accident must be higher than the cost of prevention before "rational man" is induced to act. American academic Peter Schuck extends deterrence theory to public administration. Like other economic rationalists, he argues that tort law deters wrongdoing and promotes vigorous decision-making and systemic efficiency, while at the same time providing for the compensation of victims (Schuck, 1983, pp.16–25). Economic rationalists convinced of the value of deterrence also place much emphasis on insurance. What insurers do is vital to the success of tort law in this respect. We all know that private insurers exact a penalty from careless drivers, who lose their "no claims bonus". Drivers who fall into certain risky categories may have their premiums automatically loaded. These are all attempts at deterrence but private insurers make other more sophisticated attempts to improve safety; thus they may insist on inspecting premises or require certain safety standards to be in place before they agree to accept a risk. Insurance practice will become more rational as new electronic monitoring and metering systems are introduced. Admittedly, there is no convincing evidence as to the effectiveness of these measures but then there is no convincing evidence against.

Leaving the high ground of theory, we can see that a presumption of deterrence underlies the way in which the doctrine of contributory negligence operates, especially in cases of employers' liability. Under the contributory negligence doctrine, a claimant can expect to lose a proportion of his damages in any case where he is guilty of a lack of care for his own safety. This apportionment distorts models of enterprise liability because, on the one hand, it fails to allocate to the enterprise the true cost of the accident and, on the other, any reduction in the victim's damages is a loss borne by him alone and hence not spread, in accordance with the economic theory, across a wider constituency. Contributory negligence necessarily also raises questions as to who is to be deterred: some authors believe that the employer is in the best position to prevent accidents, while others favour personal liability. The argument for non-delegable duty is that conditions of work are within the employer's control and not the employee's. A sensible strategy of deterrence would thus treat the employer as primarily responsible for workplace safety and restrain the use of contributory negligence to outrageous cases of workers' disobedience or reckless indifference to risk (Fagelson, 1979). The underlying ethos of tort law, with its heavy emphasis on individual, personal responsibility, mitigates against this solution, however. The case law tends to show that judges, who by and large continue to assume that tort law has deterrent properties, are far more likely to apportion damages according to a rough and ready assessment of "comparative fault".

A strong illustration of the judicial belief in tort law as a deterrent comes from a set of traffic accident cases decided at a time when the efficacy of seat belts in preventing serious injury was first recognised. There was, however, much parliamentary opposition to making seat belts compulsory. Unable to legislate, the Government relied on its Highway Code to advise drivers strongly to "fit seat belts and make sure they are always used". The Highway Code also adopted the awkward strategy that the use or non-use of front seat belts, which remained in principle optional, could nonetheless be used as evidence in civil proceedings. The judges then stepped in to fill the legislative gap by holding that a passenger who had contributed to his own injuries through failure to wear a seat belt should normally forfeit 25 per cent of his damages (*Froom v Butcher*, 1976).

Measured against alternatives used by the state since the first Factory Acts were passed in the nineteenth century to improve the record of workplace health and safety, the deterrent message of tort law is blunt and muted. The primary purpose of the Health and Safety at Work Act 1974, an important step in the direction of accident prevention, was not, as perhaps we have so far implied, the compensation of individuals, but the prevention of disease and accidents. The Act establishes a Health and Safety Executive to promote safety in the workplace, one of whose main functions is to encourage co-operation in accident prevention between workers, employers and, most important, unions. This is clearly something that adversarial tort actions are ill equipped to do and may actually inhibit. It is dangerous to apologise or admit to wrongdoing if expensive litigation is in the offing. In the same way, we shall find the New Zealand Accident Compensation Scheme, discussed in the final chapter, strongly emphasising prevention and rehabilitation.

One benefit of regulatory procedures is regular inspection by a trained inspectorate, again beyond the capacity of a court (Baldwin, 1987). Unlike tort law, which comes into play retrospectively and often many years after an accident has occurred, been investigated and is forgotten, the regulator is a forward-looking "fire watcher", designed to identify dangers before accidents occur. The Health and Safety Executive also possesses the power to issue "stop orders" where it finds operations or machinery to be hazardous and is not, like courts, reduced to an award of damages. Statistics superficially suggest a measure of success. The second edition of this book recorded that in 1961, there were 1228 fatal accidents annually; in 1977, when the Health and Safety Executive started to keep statistics, the figure had fallen to 763 according to its Annual Report, and deaths continued to fall, with a single upsurge attributable to a major oil rig disaster. The Annual Report for 2000–01, though compiled on a somewhat different basis, suggests that accident rates are continuing to fall: from 109.8 accidents per head of the working population in 1998–99 to 0.81 in 2003–04, 235 deaths in total.

In the absence of reliable statistics, the true deterrent effects of tort law remain a matter for conjecture. During the 1990s, the matter has been subjected to a full-scale survey undertaken at the University of Toronto, where a team of researchers reviewed the evidence and found it inconclusive. In some areas of activity, an element of deterrence can apparently be detected: for example, the introduction of a no-fault compensation scheme for victims of automobile accidents in Quebec produced an upsurge in fatal accidents. But what was the cause? One researcher argues that high-risk drivers, previously unable to secure insurance, were now on the roads; another discerns a drop in average driving standards; the arguments are endless. Overall, the authors of the Toronto survey concluded that tort law as a system of deterrence performed reasonably well only in road traffic cases (Dewes and Trebilcock, 1992). Four years later, a more ambitious survey was published. This set out to test evidence on the efficacy of the torts system and of its alternatives against the goals of deterrence, compensation, and corrective justice. Five categories of accident—traffic, medical mishap, product liability, environmental and workplace accidents—were evaluated and the impact of criminal responsibility, regulation and compensation schemes compared (Dewes, Duff and Trebilcock, 1996). The conclusion was once more that the deterrent properties of tort law were strongest for traffic accidents and weakest for environmentally related accidents. The incentive effects of the system were mixed in the case of medical and product-related accidents, where one might expect them to be highest, while in the case of workplace accidents, workers' compensation levies appear to have stronger deterrent effects than the tort system. From a compensation perspective—for the judges, tort law's main objective—the tort system appeared to fail badly in all five areas, with the failure being most severe for environmentally related, product-related, and medically induced injuries. The strongest words were reserved for medical liability cases, where the authors concluded that:

"Although distributive inequality and market failures appear to justify some form of compensation for the victims of medical injuries, civil liability is not an optimal instrument for accomplishing this objective. On the contrary, tort compensation for medical injuries is doctrinally inappropriate, procedurally inefficient, and distributively unjust. Available benefits are often excessive, but very few victims are eligible to recover at all. When it is paid, malpractice compensation is slow, insufficient and costly to administer. Finally, the manner in which malpractice insurance is generally financed achieves a regressive transfer of resources." (Dewes, Duff and Trebilcock, 1996, p.117)

Despite this robust conclusion, which provides strong support for an accident compensation plan for victims of all medical accidents, such plans exist in only a handful of countries, of which the United Kingdom is not one.

Even if there could be conclusive proof that tort law deters, there would not necessarily be agreement as to whether the effects were good or bad. In the area of medical accident, there are fears of the growth of "defensive medicine" in response to extensions of liability, while strict product liability is claimed by its critics to have a chilling effect on technological innovation and research in the related area of the pharmaceutical industry. The first Toronto study found that the fear of medical malpractice suits could manifest itself in diametrically opposite effects: it might, on the one hand, force hospitals to over-use advanced technology, one reason, it is sometimes assumed, for the increase in the number of caesarian sections; on the other hand, it might cause practitioners to abandon experimental treatment or leave areas of high-risk practice, particularly in the field of obstetrics (Dewes and Trebilcock, 1992, pp.80–83). The dangers of "over-deterrence" may be heightened by the fact that doctors apparently over-estimate the chance of being sued by a factor of about three (Harris, 1991a, p.298). In short, the effects of medical malpractice litigation cannot be accurately quantified and, more importantly, tort law cannot—as regulators can—accurately pinpoint in advance the conduct to be deterred; indeed, records of medical insurers reveal that an astonishing number of simple errors—confusion between a patient's left and right limb, for example—are recurrent. This does not suggest that they can be deterred. We need to be clear about this message when considering recent developments in actions for medical negligence—a modern growth industry—discussed in the next two chapters.

There is a wider warning in the experience of American tort law, where judges have more openly espoused victim-oriented theories of enterprise liability to extend the boundaries of tort law. Perhaps inconsistently in the light of his views on public administration, Schuck (1988) has criticised "the new ideology of tort law", which has lured courts away from tort law's simple objective of "corrective justice between the litigants" towards "a preoccupation with achieving social goals". Not only has this led to dangerous inconsistencies but it has also revealed the technical incompetence of the judiciary to deal with difficult scientific evidence, another point to bear in mind when evaluating the performance of courts in difficult medical cases turning on the evaluation of scientific and technological evidence. By moving to implement complex, economic theories of loss allocation incapable of empirical verification, courts may easily outstrip their technical competence and their constitutional legitimacy (Atiyah, 1987a, p.535).

DETERRENCE, PUNISHMENT AND VENGEANCE

"When injured people clamour for recourse against their injurers", argues Ripstein (1998), "their concern is not just with compensation, but with justice." To link tort law with fault, as the public undoubtedly does, implies that deterrence and even punishment should be amongst its goals (Schwartz, 1982). In this respect, judges and legal academics seem to be out of line with public opinion. The official position was established by Lord Devlin's famous speech in *Rookes v Barnard* (1964). Speaking for the House,

Lord Devlin constructed two simple equations: crime = punishment and tort law = compensation. This had the effect of ending, in all but a handful of exceptional tort cases, the possibility of punitive damages. According to Lord Devlin, these exceptions were (i) where an official abuses governmental power, and (ii) where the defendant has acted "contumeliously" or deliberately in defiance of the law; shortly afterwards, a further exception was admitted for defamation cases (*Broome v Cassell*, see above, p.42). *Rookes* marked a parting of the ways from the United States, where exemplary damages, typically awarded by a jury, play an important role in personal injuries and consumer class actions (Fleming, 1987, pp.101–138). Here, we shall find courts struggling to make their principles work. Somewhat unwillingly, the Law Commission, alert to the risk of "golden handshakes", admits that exemplary, though never punitive, damages are "useful in fighting a wide range of outrageously wrongful conduct, including fraud, police misconduct, infringement of health and safety standards, environmental pollution and sex and race discrimination". They have therefore recommended that exemplary damages should be available for "a legal wrong (other than breach of contract) if the defendant has deliberately and outrageously disregarded the plaintiff's rights" (Law Com.1997). But does this compromise position go far enough to retain public trust in tort law as a *corrective* justice system?

Professor Linden once famously compared tort law with an ombudsman, serving ordinary people "in their struggle for a more humane civilization by operating as an instrument of social pressure upon centres of governmental, financial and intellectual power" (Linden, 1973). It opens the doors of offices and boardrooms, exposes filing systems, reveals hidden documents, brings decision-making into the open and allows it to be scrutinised. Today we would probably express this by saying that tort law promotes transparency and accountability. Criminal justice, public inquiries and ombudsman investigations are started, run by and controlled by public officials; the tort action rests in the hands of private parties, as we saw in *Halford*. Again, in *Hill v Chief Constable of West Yorkshire* (1988), a mother sued the police in respect of the murder of her daughter by a criminal who, she claimed, could have been arrested earlier but for police negligence; as in *Halford*, the true motive was not pecuniary compensation but accountability.

In *AB v South West Water Services* (1993), a group action was brought against the water authority by inhabitants of the town of Camelford in respect of contamination of the town water supply by a spillage of aluminium sulphate. The action group claimed damages for illness and debilitation but their real anger was directed at their treatment by the water authority, which had over a long period dismissed their symptoms as neurosis, had failed to deal with them truthfully and refused to admit the spillage. For this deceitful conduct, the action group claimed exemplary and aggravated damages. After the Court of Appeal, resting on Lord Devlin's "bright line" between compensatory and punitive damages, had ruled that exemplary awards were not available in a negligence action, a critic of the judgment reproached the court for undercutting the power of civil courts to reprove anti-social conduct by defendants (Pipe, 1994, p.97). It is hard to eradicate the feeling that tort law should include an element of retribution. After the Hillsborough football disaster, for example, a settlement followed a public inquiry (Cmnd.9710, 1986). Scraton, a lawyer for the support group, publicly deplored the voluntary settlement, arguing:

"In one of the most televised, monitored and photographed disasters in the UK . . . no individual, no corporate body has had to admit even negligence. The law and the legal process will be the final victims of Hillsborough—for the loss of faith among all those involved will never be restored." (Scraton, 1992, p.7)

This reaction would certainly surprise the economic rationalist, seeking to perfect an efficient compensation system. If it seems just to compensate, why resort to litigation?

The same conflicting viewpoints underlie the decisions in the New Zealand case of *Bottrill v A* (2003), a case that challenges the monopoly of the state-funded accident compensation plan. The plaintiff developed invasive cervical cancer requiring extensive treatment after the defendant misread and misreported four cervical smear slides. His record was a poor one: he had previously misreported many other slides. The plaintiff sued in negligence for exemplary damages, arguing that if any one of the initial three slides had been correctly reported, her treatment would have been less severe and her prognosis much better. The question for the courts was whether this action could survive s.319 of the New Zealand Accident Compensation Act 2001, which expressly extinguishes the personal injuries action. The New Zealand Court of Appeal, influenced by the Camelford decision, thought that it could, but only to register condemnation of outrageous conduct or mark contumelious disregard by the defendant of the plaintiff's rights, features that they did not think were present. The Privy Council, reinstating the case for consideration of the facts, ruled that exemplary damages could be available in a negligence action if the conduct complained of was sufficiently outrageous and if the judge felt the case called for public condemnation. The judges seem to have difficulty in making up their minds.

But does this use of tort law represent a public-spirited quest for accountability or is it, as Linden (1969, p.1021) once suggested, merely a legal means of wreaking vengeance? We are fast following the United States to become a very litigious society, where problems are increasingly sorted out in court: schoolchildren go to court to complain that they have been bullied; rough play on the sports field provokes litigation from other players, aggrieved that their opponents have escaped punishment through the disciplinary procedures. Law is being used in situations previously handled privately by the community. In the sphere of public law, litigation is used to circumvent political action or as a substitute for alternative, public law remedies, a process accelerated recently by the introduction of the Human Rights Act (Hedley, 1994). In the United States, where the use of tort law to vindicate constitutional rights is more familiar, a public law theory of "corrective justice" has been advanced in explanation:

"Systems of rights are premised on the concept of individual entitlements to personal security and autonomy-entitlements that may not usually be overridden or compromised for the good of society. Tortious conduct, whether defined by moral, political or economic criteria, constitutes a wrongful infringement of those entitlements. From a rights-oriented standpoint, then, the role of the tort system is to perform 'corrective justice' in order to preserve entitlements against wrongful infringement. The fundamental tenet of such corrective justice is that wrongdoers should make their victims whole." (Rosenberg, 1984, p.875)

Less idealistic is Atiyah's picture of the "blame culture", in which people have a strong financial incentive to blame others for loss or death or wrongful injury (Atiyah, 1997, p.138).

The complexity of tort law, where multiple objectives have to be fitted into a simple, bipolar framework, presents the judges with insoluble problems. Discussing the unsuccessful action in the *Hill* case (above) the legal philosopher, Ishtak England (1993, p.190), points to the difficulty of reconciling the different objectives of a system in which:

"Public law and private law, distributive justice and corrective justice, intermingle in a complementary way. The specific weight to be given to each domain in concrete circumstances is a matter of controversy, and the contrasting judicial decisions reflect the inherent difficulty in accommodating the conflicting aims."

Another academic writer says that:

"Tort law is about compensating those who are wrongfully injured. But even more fundamentally it is about recognising and righting wrongful conduct by one person or a group of persons that harms others. If tort law becomes incapable of recognising important wrongs, and hence incapable of righting them, victims will be left with a sense of grievance and the public will be left with a feeling that justice is not what it should be." (McLachlin, 1998, p.16)

Let us make this the last word.

FURTHER READING

A "must read" is Hutchinson and Morgan, "The Canengusian Connection: A Kaleidoscope of Tort Theory" (1984) 22 *Osgoode Hall Law Journal* 69, a mock report of the running down case of *Allan v Derek*, decided in the Supreme Court of Canengus on April 1, 1984 by a judicial panel inspired by different tort law theories. Almost equally palatable, *if* you can get hold of a rare copy, is W. Friedmann's classic, *Law in a Changing Society* (Harmondsworth, Pelican, 1971). A more classical approach is that of Cane, "Justice and Justifications For Tort Liability" (1982) 2 *Oxford Journal of Legal Studies* 30. Cane took his ideas further in an ambitious attempt to reclassify torts in *An Anatomy of Tort Law* (Oxford, Hart Publishing, 1997), a useful alternative to textbooks. J. Conaghan and R. Mansell, *The Wrongs of Tort* (2nd ed., London, Pluto Press, 1993), apply the critical legal approach to English law. Schwartz, "The Beginning and the Possible End of the Rise of Modern American Tort Law" (1992) 26 *Georgia Law Review* 601 is a good introduction to the progression of twentieth-century tort law, as is England, "The System Builders: A Critical Appraisal of Modern American Tort Theory" (1980) 9 *Journal of Legal Studies* 27. Economic theory is easily accessible in Posner's textbook, *Economic Analysis of Law* (5th ed., Boston, Little Brown, 1992). A good introduction to economic analysis is also given by Veljanovski, *The Economics of Law—An Introductory Text* (London, Institute of Economic Affairs, 1990), which contains an excellent explanation of the "Learned Hand" formula. Rosenberg speaks up for tort law in a difficult article, "The Causal Connection in Mass Exposure Cases: A Public Law Vision of the Tort System" (1984) 97 *Harvard Law Review* 851. R. Abel speaks against it in "Torts", in *The Politics of Law, A Progressive Critique* (Kairys ed., New York, Pantheon, 1982). Linden, "Tort Law as Ombudsman" (1973) 51 *Canadian Bar Review* 155 is a good read but you should also read his "Reconsidering Tort Law as Ombudsman", in *Issues in Tort Law* (Steel and Rodgers-Magnet ed., Toronto, Carswell, 1983). Atiyah's 1970 classic is now edited by P. Cane, *Atiyah's Accidents, Compensation and the Law* (6th ed., London, Butterworths, 1999). But Atiyah's view's have changed dramatically. You can find them in P. Atiyah, *The Damages Lottery* (Oxford, Hart Publishing, 1997). Even if you do not agree with Atiyah's conclusions, *The Damages Lottery* is an excellent introduction to the troubled area of accident compensation.

3

THE RISE AND RISE OF NEGLIGENCE

In 1932, a young man made legal history by buying a bottle of ginger beer in a small shop in Paisley. The story must have sounded rather absurd in the grandiose surroundings of the House of Lords. The young man had bought the bottle to make an ice-cream soda for his friend. She drank some, but when he was refilling her glass, what seemed to be the corpse of a long-dead snail apparently fell out of the opaque bottle. The young lady suffered a shock and also an upset stomach. What was the legal position?

If the young man had sued the shopkeeper in contract, the story of tort law might have been very different, because he, if he could prove his story, would have been entitled to a return of the price he had paid. But he had suffered no physical injury and it was the young woman who was now claiming damages from the manufacturer for the nausea and shock suffered. The claim was so novel that the House of Lords was asked to rule before the trial of the action whether it could be entertained. The House ruled that there could in principle be liability in negligence. (The presence or absence of the snail was never finally established because the case never came to trial.) The famous passage in which Lord Atkin outlined his reasoning has become the cornerstone of modern tort law:

"The liability for negligence, whether you style it such or treat it as in other systems as a species of 'culpa' [fault], is no doubt based upon a general public sentiment of moral wrongdoing for which the offender must pay. But acts or omissions which any moral code would censure cannot in a practical world be treated so as to give a right to every person injured by them to demand relief. In this way rules of law arise which limit the range of complainants and the extent of their remedy. The rule that you are to love your neighbour becomes in law: You must not injure your neighbour, and the lawyer's question: Who is my neighbour? receives a restricted reply. You must take reasonable care to avoid acts or omissions which you can reasonably foresee would be likely to injure your neighbour. Who then, in law, is my neighbour? The answer seems to be persons who are so closely and directly affected by my act that I ought reasonably to have them in contemplation as being so affected when I am directing my mind to the acts or omissions which are called in question." (*Donoghue v Stevenson*, 1932)

In deciding that the manufacturer was liable outside the terms of his contracts, to people with whom he had no direct relationship, the House greatly extended the range of people who could sue. By holding the manufacturer rather than the retailer primarily responsible for the safety of goods circulated, the House of Lords produced a doctrine in tune with twentieth-century commercial practices and laid the foundation of what today we call "products liability" (see above, p.14). But the case was to have a much wider effect on tort law. Lord Atkin's judgment does not speak only of manufacturers, producers or consumers; it is couched in general terms and can be read as a general statement of principle, outlining the circumstances in which one person will incur legal liability to another for his or her acts or omissions. Something about the directness and simplicity of the language of the famous "neighbour" passage gave it a wide appeal that caused it to be read in precisely this fashion.

Lord Atkin's neighbour test remains today the basis on which civil liability for negligence is measured, although, as we shall see later, the way in which the test is formulated has undergone some changes. When broken down, Lord Atkin's test is found to consist of three elements: duty, breach and damage. Civil liability for negligence is incurred whenever:

1. A "neighbour" relationship exists such that the defendant can reasonably foresee that his acts will affect the plaintiff. (Today this relationship is usually described as one of "proximity".) And

2. The defendant has failed to take reasonable care. And

3. The defendant's acts or omissions have caused damage to the plaintiff. Today this damage must be reasonably foreseeable by the defendant (see below, p.66).

Of the hundreds of cases in which these principles have been discussed, the majority merely provide illustrations of the way in which the courts are likely to behave in applying them. They are twigs, which can be snapped off without spoiling the shape of the tree. The handful of cases that remain contain important extensions to the principle, which allow the tort of negligence to spread into new areas. They are the branches of the tree of negligence.

Many of the duties imposed by the law of negligence either existed before *Donoghue* was decided or were fairly easily established. It is, for example, self-evident that road users owe a duty of care to other road users; the existence and basis of this duty does not need to be argued in one case after another and counsel in running-down cases do not have to start by citing Lord Atkin to the judge. The *extent* of the duty may, however, be less clear: the courts have not been very happy to extend liability to bystanders who have not actually been physically injured in a traffic accident but who have suffered shock as a consequence of the accident (*McLoughlin v O'Brian*, 1983; *Bourhill v Young*, 1943). Even when nervous shock had been admitted as a cause of action, the extent of the duty posed problems: should liability extend to all bystanders or was it restricted to relatives of the injured? And did the victim have to witness the accident with his or her own eyes or was it enough if he or she was told about it? This is one of the most problematic areas of modern tort law and we shall return to it later in the chapter.

In other cases, it proved less simple to establish a general duty. We know from the last chapter that negligence originated as a set of specific duties recognised by the common law, which came together inside the tort of negligence. We know too that just such a duty, non-delegable in character, now rests on employers to look after the safety of their employees. The courts, however, took a long time to arrive at this position because of a serious obstacle to co-ordination. The unfortunate precedent of *Priestley v Fowler* (1837) established the doctrine of "common employment", according to which a master was not vicariously liable for injury caused by one servant to another. This doctrine, which severely limited the growth of vicarious liability, was finally eliminated by Parliament, but not before 1948. How would the courts surmount this obstacle? A first resort was Factories Acts which, as we saw earlier, often imposed obligations on employers to guard against specific hazards, sometimes providing for criminal liability. These could be used to impose civil liability for breach of statutory duty (*Groves v Lord Wimborne*, 1898). But once *Donoghue* had been decided, it was possible to evade the doctrine of common employment in a less roundabout way. The employer's duty could be reformulated as a *primary* duty of care. The House of Lords took this step in *Wilsons and Clyde Coal Co v English* (1938). This case established a threefold duty of care to provide workers with (i) a competent work force; (ii) adequate plant and equipment; and (iii) a proper system of working, with competent and effective supervision. The separate and highly specific statutory duties imposed on employers could now be linked behind the facade of negligence and presented as a variant of negligence liability in which statutory duties operate to show a breach of duty and establish an appropriate standard of care (Glanville Williams, 1960). The courts had come a long way in a century, although they could of course have moved much faster with the co-operation of Parliament.

The concept of a primary duty of care that is "non-delegable" and independent of wrongdoing by other actors, remaining in place whether or not they have been negligent, has become a linchpin of our modern law of negligence. It first showed its usefulness in medical cases, where it meant that, rather than trying to pin blame on an individual nurse or doctor, which is manifestly difficult, a claimant could succeed if it could be shown that the hospital authorities were operating an unsafe system. Equally, it was useful in dealing with cases where the actors were not in an employer–employee relationship, when the common law doctrine of vicarious liability did not apply; a sharp distinction existed between "employees", for whom the employer was vicariously liable and "independent contractors", for whom the liability was limited to careful selection of a reputable and appropriately qualified contractor. On building sites, where small operators are not properly insured or have gone out of business, the chance of reparation may turn on whether a court will impose a non-delegable duty of care on the site-owner or main contractor (*Ferguson v Welsh*, 1987); the same is true of hospitals staffed by agency nurses, where the courts first extended the doctrine of vicarious liability (*Gold v Essex CC*, 1942) but then took the more convenient route of laying a duty on the health authority to provide a competent *system* of care.

Today, establishing a duty to guard against death or serious personal injury is relatively uncontroversial—except where the controversial subject of nervous shock is involved. Property loss is a little more difficult and economic loss has proved more problematic still. The key case that allowed negligence liability to be extended to economic losses and negligent advice was *Hedley Byrne v Heller & Partners Ltd* (1964). A firm of advertising agents (HB) asked a bank (H) whether one of its clients, with whom they intended doing business, was creditworthy. The reply, stated to be "without responsibility on our part", was that the client was trustworthy. When HB lost money through the client firm's liquidation they sought to recoup themselves from the bankers who, they maintained, had been negligent. But the rule of common law had always been that only fraudulent misstatements gave rise to liability. The House of Lords was being asked to perform a U-turn. The willing Law Lords gave different grounds for the decision. Lord Reid saw the duty as based on reliance, which created a "special relationship" between the parties. Lord Devlin's formulation was more restrictive. He saw the special relationship as closely related to contract: a contract that, in other words, was not quite a contract. The momentous decision which, like *Donoghue*, blurred the boundaries of contract law and tort, was radically to affect the growth of tort law. In a society whose main activities are commercial, it opened the door to claims for financial loss and paved the way too for claims in respect of professional negligence.

The case that sounded warning bells in Whitehall was, however, still to come. In *Home Office v Dorset Yacht Co Ltd* (1970) a group of Borstal boys was encamped on an island in Poole Harbour as part of a training exercise. One night they eluded their officers and boarded a yacht on which to escape to the mainland. There was a collision with the plaintiffs' yacht, which was badly damaged. Sued in its capacity as ultimate authority in charge of prisons, the Home Office advanced three arguments against liability: (i) that there is no vicarious liability in English law other than that of master and servant; (ii) that public policy required prison officers to be immune from liability; and (iii) that there were no precedents for liability. All these arguments failed.

The *Dorset Yacht* case was certainly of symbolic importance in that it demolished the virtual immunity of the Home Office, which derived from the historical immunity of the Crown from liability in tort, virtually ended by the Crown Proceedings Act 1947. A further important factor in the *Dorset Yacht* case was the emphasis placed on the flexible notion of "control". This was to open up the restrictive concept of vicarious liability, allowing the master/servant test to be circumvented. As we shall see in Ch.8, it opened the way to a flood of actions against public authorities, with the argument that they owe a primary duty of care to protect the vulnerable against risk of injury by third parties, based on statutory duties or powers that they exercise. All these developments are greatly facilitated by the *Dorset Yacht* case, which installed negligence as the general principle of civil liability. Describing *Donoghue* as a "milestone" and Lord Atkin's "neighbour" speech as a "statement of principle", Lord Reid continued:

"It is not to be treated as if it were a statutory definition. It will require qualification in new circumstances. But I think the time has come when we can and should say that it ought to apply unless there is some justification or valid explanation for its exclusion."

Negligence had come of age.

Eight years later, Lord Wilberforce took the process a stage further in *Anns v Merton LBC* (1978). The case involved the liability of a local authority for the negligent use (or perhaps a negligent failure to use) statutory powers to inspect the foundations of new buildings. A two-stage test was formulated by Lord Wilberforce to be used by judges uncertain whether or not a duty of care was owed:

- Stage 1 requires the judge to ask whether a sufficiently close relationship exists between the parties for the defendant to have foreseen that the plaintiff would be affected. This is simply a test of "proximity", a different formulation of Lord Atkin's "neighbour" test.

- Stage 2 requires the judge to ask whether any policy reason exists against the imposition of liability.

For a time, this two-stage test became the general test for duty of care in any case where the duty was novel or not self-evident. As we shall see, a point came later when the judiciary wished to move back to a less expansive formula.

THE REASONABLE MAN AND BREACH OF DUTY

As restrictions on the duty concept, the classical regulator of negligence, were gradually lifted, as immunities from liability fell and negligence emerged as the general principle of liability, the flexible and easily manipulated concepts of "proximity" and "reasonable foresight" gained ground as the central tests for liability. It is, however, important not to lose sight of the fact that negligence consists of *three* elements: duty, breach and damage. To establish a duty of care in negligence does not necessarily mean the duty has been breached. The plaintiff must also show that the defendant has fallen below the standard of care acceptable to the courts.

What is that standard? And is it subjective or objective? It would be both unfortunate and unfair if someone were to be exempted from liability because he or she was particularly clumsy, stupid or careless. The standard had to be objective. It evolved as one of commonsense or "reasonableness", once depicted through the picturesque metaphor of "the man on the Clapham omnibus". In principle, no one is allowed to fall below this standard; a learner driver, for example, should not be allowed to argue that she has caused an accident because of her inexperience (*Nettleship v Weston*, 1971). A few modern cases imply exceptions: in *Herrington* (see above, p.19), it was suggested that more in the way of precautions could be expected of a large landowner with ample resources than of a small, less well-resourced landowner, but this remains an exceptional case.

MEDICAL NEGLIGENCE

Because doctors routinely make life and death decisions and treatment that goes wrong may seriously worsen the health of a claimant, medical cases rank as the most important branch of professional negligence. They place judges in a quandary. On the one hand, a vulnerable victim merits compensation; on the other hand, negligence is fault and fault, it has been argued, is generally perceived as wrongdoing. In *Nettleship*, the frightening example was considered of an inexperienced eye surgeon who blinds a patient—apparently a common occurrence during training. Clearly there are difficulties here with the *Nettleship* test. The alternative standard applied is that of a doctor who "has acted in accordance with a practice accepted as proper by a responsible body of medical men skilled in that particular art". This, the so-called "*Bolam* test", has for many years governed liability in medical negligence cases (*Bolam v Friern Hospital Management Committee*, 1957).

A finding of wrongdoing has repercussions not only for doctors' pockets—this can for a premium be insured against—but more importantly for his or her career. Even the threat of liability may be sufficient to act as a negative deterrent, causing medical practitioners to operate with one eye on the courts, and to become over-cautious. Shortage of midwives and specialist gynaecological services is sometimes blamed on fear of liability in a risk-prone area of practice. In Britain, the rapid rise in caesarian sections is blamed on the fear of litigation: doctors are afraid to allow natural deliveries because, if the child suffers birth trauma, they may be sued. Although such reasoning sounds alarmist, there is, as we saw in the last chapter, some empirical evidence to support it.

For two main reasons, tort law was at first highly restrictive. First, it was felt that the charitable status of hospitals merited immunity from liability; funds raised for charitable purposes should not be disbursed as damages (*Hillyer v St Bartholomew's Hospital (Governors)*, 1909). It was not until the institution of a national health service that this immunity was gradually dismantled (*Cassidy v Ministry of Health*, 1951). Secondly, the liability of medical personnel was restricted to the point that early case law suggested a standard of gross or grave negligence for medical cases, while the *Bolam* test (above) precluded the judge from personally evaluating a doctor's conduct provided that it was in tune with a body of respectable professional opinion, thus keeping liability firmly in professional hands. Lord Denning M.R. articulated the judge's dilemma in *Roe v Minister of Health* (1954), where the claimant had been paralysed when hair cracks in a glass ampoule of anaesthetic allowed leakage. The possibility that such an accident could happen had only just been uncovered by research:

"It is easy to be wise after the event and to condemn as negligence that which was only a misadventure. We ought always to be on our guard against it, especially in cases against hospitals and doctors. Medical science has conferred great benefits on mankind, but these benefits are attended by considerable risks. Every surgical operation is attended by risks. We cannot take the benefits without taking the risks. Every advance in technique is also attended by risks. Doctors, like the rest of us, have to learn by experience; and experience often teaches in a hard way ... We must not look at the 1947 accident with 1954 spectacles."

In *Whitehouse v Jordan* (1980), where a baby suffered brain damage as the consequence of a forceps delivery, Lord Denning M.R. retained his protective stance, reasoning that a "mere error of judgment" by a doctor was not to be equated with negligence. Although the House of Lords corrected Lord Denning and held that the same standard of negligence applied to doctors as to the rest of the world—a very considerable breakthrough—they did not reverse the finding that the doctor was not liable. Is there an argument for compensating every mother whose baby has brain damage from a forceps delivery? Or should we look at the matter through different spectacles and argue that advances in medical science have saved the child, when previously mother and child might both have died? Profound questions of this type should be reserved for government and parliaments—unlikely as they are to express their views!

The next step was taken in the leading case of *Sidaway v Bethlem Royal Hospital* (1985), which imported the American doctrine of "informed consent". Mrs S had been paralysed in the course of an operation to relieve stiffness. Her lawyers argued that she had not been warned of the 1–2 per cent risk of paralysis; had she known, she would never have consented to the operation. The House of Lords was divided on the extent to which patients should be informed of risk but gave cautious support to Lord Bridge's proposition that, "when questioned by a patient of apparently sound mind about risks involved in a particular treatment proposed, the doctor's duty must ... be to answer both truthfully and as fully as the questioner desires". Because the *Bolam* test remained applicable, the outcome was unfavourable to Mrs S. But *Sidaway* opened up the field of medical negligence, making it easier to sue. The defence of consent had been eroded, with the consequence that doctors have to pay more attention to their patients' wishes.

Courts are naturally moved by the plight of victims of medical accidents and wish to help the victim to victory, a sentiment that has gained impetus from decreased public trust in medical professionals. Inquiries into medical malpractice have proliferated and medical malpractice suits have increased, a trend imported from the more litigious United States. The scope of duty in medical cases has been vastly extended. The standard of care has also changed and the *Bolam* test has been modified to give judges more latitude. Perhaps the best way to describe the current relationship of judges to doctors is as one of modified deference and extended supervision, as Lord Browne-Wilkinson explains:

"In cases involving, as they so often do, the weighing of risks against benefits, the judge before accepting a body of opinion as being responsible, reasonable or respectable, will need to be satisfied that, in forming their views, the experts have directed their minds to the question of comparative risks and benefits and have reached a defensible conclusion on the matter ... at least to the extent that the practice on which the defendant is relying must, in the eyes of the court, be reasonable or have a 'logical basis'." (*Bolitho v City and Hackney Health Authority*, 1997)

Matters of life and death are today routinely referred to courts. They puzzle over "wrongful birth" cases, where parents seek to charge negligent hospital authorities with the expenses of child rearing after an unplanned pregnancy follows an unsuccessful sterilisation (*Cattanach v Melchior*, 2003; *Rees v Darlington Memorial Hospital NHS Trust*, 2003). As we shall see in the next chapter, they struggle with expert evidence and legal doctrines of causation, which they are ill equipped to understand.

CREEPING NEGLIGENCE

The expansive tort of negligence sparked off an explosion of American tort law during the 1960s and 1970s, which gradually spread through the common law world. Courts were suddenly faced with controversial civil suits. Actions were brought against rapists and murderers, by burglars injured on the job, but also against the police, who had failed to prevent the crimes (*Hill v Chief Constable of West Yorkshire*, 1988). One by one, classic immunities from liability have fallen. Lawyers are now in principle liable for their professional negligence (*Rondel v Worsley*, 1969; *Arthur S. Hall & Co v Simons*, 2000). A duty of care has been imposed on ambulance teams and the fire service, where previously only limited duties would have been thought appropriate for rescue services (*John Munroe (Acrylics) Ltd v London Fire and Civil Defence Authority*, 1996; *Capital & Counties plc v Hampshire CC*, 1997). A line of recent cases overrides the established common law principle that sportsmen are deemed to consent to normal risks: a school where sports are compulsory may be responsible for sporting injuries (*Van Oppen v Clerk to the Bedford Charity Referee*, 1990) and the duty of care has been extended to referees (*Vowles v Evans*, 2003). The British Boxing Board of Control, as the body responsible for regulating and supervising safety at boxing matches, has been held liable for the extent of injuries suffered by a boxer, allegedly due to the absence at the ringside of qualified medical attendants (*Watson v British Boxing Board of Control*, 2001). Classes of public servants previously immune from liability for public policy reasons are regularly sued. The Limitation Acts have been undermined by actions filed many years after the event, so that a Law Commission consultation paper now proposes a "long stop" period of 30 years in personal injuries cases (Law Com.151b, 1997). "Forum shopping" by litigants to move cases into the legal system most likely to provide compensation has been condoned (*Lubbe v Cape plc*, 20 July 2000).

Querying the way in which negligence principles are "worked through" and applied in novel areas, Jane Stapleton (1994) criticised many of these developments. She instanced:

- the tendency to base liability on failure by one party to "control" another;

- changed attitudes to liability for omissions;

- a new attitude to the responsibilities of property owners, extending both the ambit and scope of the duties owed;

- a judicial propensity to impose liability for failure to warn of risks, sometimes even when these are blindingly obvious;

- the growing practice of allowing intermediary parties to be "leapfrogged", changing the boundaries of tort and contract;

- a trend to transfer liability from primary to secondary actors, associated with changes in the law of vicarious liability; the conflation of the employer's primary and secondary liability; and imposition of non-delegable duties of care on corporate bodies and public authorities.

The trends had in common that they "deflect attention away from the party or parties directly and principally responsible for the damage" (Stapleton, 1995b, p.312) with the consequence that the element of fault and blame in the traditional "corrective justice" model of tort law was fast being eroded. A flood unforeseen by the judiciary and one that they began to find unwelcome had been produced. The deterrent effects of tort law may prove unpopular when playgrounds and sports facilities close down, allegedly because local authorities cannot meet standards of safety required by courts, or teachers refuse supervisory duties for fear of being sued. The American academic Peter Schuck (1988) makes similar points:

"Courts have enlarged the concept of 'action', a traditional pre-requisite for liability, to encompass inaction. In this way, they have placed individuals under a legal duty to help strangers in many situations, thereby hauling new kinds of relationships (and non-relationships) into the net of legal liability. They have accorded legal protection to new categories of interests ... They have extended the domain in time and space over which defendants' duties apply by imposing responsibility for risks that eventuate long after dependents acted and, in some toxic tort cases, for risks that were scientifically unknowable at that time. They have accepted relatively weak claims of causation ... They have routinely ignored or overridden express contractual limitations on tort liability, as well as implicit agreements by parties to allocate risk between themselves. They have abandoned or severely curtailed longstanding charitable, governmental, and familial immunities from tort liability."

A SWING OF THE PENDULUM

To summarise the argument so far, the theme that dominated the development of tort law in the second half of the twentieth century was the consolidation of the negligence principle. As tort law seemed to the judges to be developing as the main system of accident compensation, the duty of care concept was rapidly expanded. The period of greatest expansion for tort law in the United Kingdom was the early 1970s, when negligence came of age as the general principle of civil liability, to the end of the 1980s, when recessive economic theories became fashionable and the welfare state entered a period of decline. From the time of *Donoghue*, when isolated islands of negligence liability floated amongst the nominate torts, we had reached the point of islands of immunity floating against the tide in a sea of negligence (Smith and Burns, 1982).

In recent years, however, the tide has begun to turn, with a sharp move back in the direction from which Lords Reid and Wilberforce had helped negligence to emerge in *Dorset Yacht* and *Anns*. A "conservative vision for the overall reach of tort law" has prevailed (Stapleton, 1994) and a new spirit of pragmatism and incrementalism now governs negligence liability. A first step in the move to restrain the growth of negligence was an attack on the two-stage *Anns* test (above) in two leading cases heard by the Privy Council and House of Lords. In *Yuen Kun-yeu v Attorney*

General of Hong Kong (1978), Lord Keith dismissed the test as "having been elevated to a degree of importance greater than it merits, and greater perhaps than its author intended". Undercutting the concept of negligence as a *general principle*, Lord Oliver added that "to search for any single formula which will serve as a general test of liability is to pursue a will-o'-the wisp". In the later case of *Caparo v Dickman* (1990), Lord Bridge described the *Anns* test as both impractical and unsuitable as a general test for the existence of a duty of care. The House of Lords in *Caparo* introduced a new, three-stage test for duty:

- Stage 1 requires the judge to ask himself whether there is a "relationship of proximity" between the parties;

- Stage 2 requires the judge to satisfy himself that the loss, damage or injury was reasonably foreseeable;

- Stage 3 requires him to ask himself whether it is "fair, just and reasonable" to impose liability.

Broadly, the new approach reverses the burden of establishing a new duty, laying it firmly on the claimant who seeks to establish duty. In a plea for "incrementalism", Lord Bridge exhorted lower courts to attach "greater significance to the more traditional cate-gorisations as guides to the existence, the scope and the limits of the varied duties of care which the law imposes". Later, Lord Hoffmann was to underscore this advice, instructing courts first to consider those cases where a duty already exists and then to ask whether there were "considerations of analogy, policy, fairness and justice for extending it to cover a new situation" (*Stovin v Wise*, 1996). Both tests are negative and incremental.

Both *Yuen Kun-yeu* and *Caparo* were cases of economic loss: the first concerned the liability of a registrar of financial institutions for loss allegedly caused to depositors by failure properly to exercise his supervisory powers; the second concerned the liability of audi-tors to investors relying on audited accounts when purchasing shares. So we should probably not deduce from these two cases that the victim-oriented trend in personal injuries litigation will be easy to reverse. Indeed, the High Court of Australia, adding sec-ondary criteria to sharpen the "fair, just and reasonable" formula, has stressed that the vulnerability of an individual or ascertainable class of persons "is a significant factor in establishing a duty of care" (*Perre v Apand*, 1999).

It is, on the one hand, undoubtedly less fashionable for the superior courts to connive at litigants' attempts to reach for the deepest pockets. They no longer view the tort system as a vehicle for the automatic transfer of losses. Yet paradoxically, parallel courts have shown themselves willing to dismantle a number of established immunities, illustrated in cases summarised above. At the doctrinal level, we are fast moving away from narrow relationships of proximity as the basis of negligence liability and drifting towards a position where nearly everyone seems to owe a duty of care to everyone else in every situation. As duty of care abandons its role as the primary control factor in the negligence action, so the focal point shifts from duty to breach. In the next chapter, we shall see causation emerge as a significant regulator of liability and a shift in interest to remoteness of damage, the third element in the tort of negligence. Whether or not they are beneficial, these swings are certainly confusing.

FURTHER READING

Two essays by Weir, "The Staggering March of Negligence" and Stapleton, "Duty of Care Factors: A Selection from the Judicial Menu", in *The Law of Obligations: Essays in Celebration of John Fleming* (Cane and Stapleton ed., Oxford, Clarendon, 1998) are specially relevant to the theme of this chapter. The classic account is Stapleton's earlier article, "The Gist of Negligence" (1988) 104 *Law Quarterly Review* 213 and 389. A rather different approach to the process of ebb and flow is that of Schwartz, "The Beginning and the Possible End of the Rise of Modern American Tort Law" (1992) 26 *Georgia Law Review* 601. This focuses on the United States but the themes recur in other common law jurisdictions. For an attempt to draw principled "bright lines", see Stapleton, "The Condition of the Law of Tort", in *The Frontiers of Liability III* (Birks ed., Oxford, Oxford University Press, 1994). A simple doctrinal explanation of the retreat from *Anns* is Kidner "Resiling from the *Anns* Principle: The Variable Nature of Proximity in Negligence" (1983) 7 *Legal Studies* 319. The case for incrementalism is well presented by Smith and Burns, "Donoghue v Stevenson—The Not So Golden Anniversary" (1983) 46 *Modern Law Review* 147.

4

FACING THE CONSEQUENCES

"For want of a nail, the shoe was lost,
For want of a shoe, the horse was lost,
For want of a horse, the rider was lost,
For want of the rider, the battle was lost,
For want of the battle, the kingdom was lost
And all for the want of a horseshoe nail."

Nursery rhyme

In the last chapter, we focused on the first two elements of a negligence action: duty of care and breach of duty. For a negligence action to be successful, there is a third prerequisite: the claimant must show that *damage* has been suffered. Today, damage must also be *foreseeable*. In practice, a single act of negligence may have disastrous and unforeseen consequences, making it impractical to hold the defendant liable for all the damage flowing from his act. (Although an omission to act can also be a ground for liability, the common law has always found difficulty in accepting that loss can be caused by an omission to act, a prejudice only just beginning to disperse.) Especially where economic loss is concerned, courts try to avoid making a single defendant liable to "an indeterminate class of persons for indeterminate sums". In trying to spread the load, they look for a cut-off point, asking the question "For what damage and for what losses is the defendant *not* to be held responsible?" In answering this deceptively simple question, English courts currently rely heavily on the three interlocking principles of *causation*, *foreseeability* and *remoteness*. Arguably, a better way in some cases would be to apportion responsibility, as American courts are starting to do in complex products liability cases, according to the defendant's "market share" in distribution. Gradually, the outcome of apportionment is becoming more acceptable but, as this chapter will show, there is still a long way to go.

The common law rules about causation were simple and severe. First, the burden of proof lay on the claimant to prove on a balance of probabilities that the defendant caused his injury. It can be difficult to establish the facts. Take the textbook example of a shooting party, where a ricocheting bullet injures someone (*Cook v Lewis*, 1951). If the claimant cannot prove who fired the fatal shot, he fails. This outcome seems unjust. The claimant has certainly not caused his injuries; the shooting party is responsible. All should make a contribution to the damages, which ought, in other words, to be apportioned. The common law rules about apportionment also tended to be simple and severe. Where the claimant's act was partly responsible for the damage, the harsh rule was that the person who had the "last chance" to avoid damage had to bear responsibility for it.

In a rare burst of parliamentary activity, the doctrine of contributory negligence was finally substituted by the Law Reform (Contributory Negligence) Act 1945. The Act provides that the court may *apportion responsibility* between the parties, reducing the damages of a claimant who has "contributed to his own injuries" by the amount that "a court thinks just and equitable having regard to [his] share in the responsibility for the damage". This power is widely used today, especially in traffic and workplace accident cases. When the Act speaks of "contribution", however, it refers only to the relationship between the two parties to the case. Thus the apportionment that it can achieve is limited. Where several defendants have all made some contribution to the damage, each one is separately liable to the claimant for *all* the resultant damage although, between the wrongdoers, the share of responsibility can be apportioned. This time the severe rule benefits the claimant by leaving him with the choice whether to sue *all* the defendants as jointly liable or only one, in which case it is up to the defendant to join the contributors as parties to the proceedings in order to obtain apportionment.

Causation has always been central to the common law, as we can see from the old trespass case of *Scott v Shepherd* (1773). S1 threw a lighted firework into a crowded market, which landed on Y's stall. W picked it up and threw it across the market, where it landed on R's stall. R did the same, but this time the firework hit S2, the plaintiff, in the face, exploded and blinded him. The traditional common law answer to the question "Who was responsible for the damage caused?" is probably S1—the court actually split on the question of whether this was a trespass or negligence action—but there are several alternative answers:

- S1 is responsible. His negligent act started the chain of actions that led directly to the plaintiff's injury. All the intervening acts were foreseeable and reasonable attempts to avoid the damage. They did not break the "chain of causation".

- S1 is not responsible. The "chain of causation" has been broken by new intervening actors, making the damage too remote.

- R, the immediate actor, is responsible. His act is a battery. It is the "direct" cause of injury. He had the "last chance" to avoid the accident.

- S, W and R have all contributed to the accident. Their acts were negligent and their share of responsibility will need to be apportioned.

CAUSATION IN FACT: THE "BUT FOR" TEST

Like many academic writers, Jane Stapleton deplores the imprecise and vague language that has bedevilled the topic of causation. She identifies two quite separate inquiries that must be made. These, she believes, are often hopelessly entangled:

1. Was the breach of duty by the defendant part of the history that led to the deleterious outcome of which the claimant complains? (Causation in fact)

2. Should the relevant consequence be held to be within the appropriate scope of liability for the consequences of the tortious conduct? (Causation in law) (Stapleton, 2002).

In trying to answer question 1, generations of students have been taught to put their faith in the "but for" test, which poses the question slightly differently: Would the damage have occurred "but for" the defendant's act? This test is sometimes helpful in isolating an act that is *not* causative. In *Barnett v Chelsea Hospital* (1968), for example, a patient went to the casualty department complaining of vomiting after drinking a cup of tea. The duty doctor told him to go home and take an aspirin, and some hours later he died of arsenic poisoning. His widow sued. Perhaps surprisingly, the action failed the "but for" test. Despite the obviously inadequate diagnosis and treatment, the hospital successfully argued that, by the time the deceased saw the doctor, no treatment could have been effective. This type of argument can work in reverse. A patient goes to casualty after a traffic accident for stitches in a minor wound. The doctor prescribes antibiotics without taking the elementary precaution of ascertaining whether the patient is allergic. The patient dies. Here the treatment and not the original accident was the cause of death, because it was arguably so negligent as to "break the chain of causation". "But for" the doctor's intervention, the patient would not have died. To rephrase this in legal language, a "new intervening act" has rendered the original cause of damage too "remote".

The "but for" test is, however, an unreliable guide, to be inserted like a comma where the judge thinks fit. In the controversial case of *McWilliams v Sir William Arrol* (1962), a steeplejack had fallen and been gravely injured while climbing a tall chimney. At the time of the accident, he was not, as he should have been, wearing a safety belt. There were no safety belts on the site. The employers' explanation was that the belts had been taken away because steeplejacks refused to wear them even when they were provided. Applying the "but for" test gives the answer that "but for" the absence of the belt, the steeplejack would not have fallen, but takes us no further. As the judge put it, "any disputed question of causation (factual or legal) will involve a number of factual events or conditions which satisfy the 'but for' test. A process of evaluation and selection has then to take place." These were the possible deductions:

1.   The steeplejack could not have worn a belt because there was no belt available. The employers owe a legal duty of care to their workers to provide belts. They are liable.

2.   The belts are not on the site because the workers would not have worn them if they had been there. The steeplejack is the cause of his own accident. "But for" his refusal to wear a safety belt, the steeplejack would never have fallen. Controversially, this is the way the judge decided the case.

3.   The employer is the "cause" of the accident as in (1) but has a total defence of *consent*. The steeplejack understands the risk of working without a safety belt but prefers to climb without one. He has accepted the risk. Today, courts are not inclined to use this defence against workers except in unusual cases.

4.   Finally, and today the most common answer, the courts may apportion the blame between the claimant and defendant, using the partial defence of contributory negligence.

Reflect on the different attitudes to compensation and deterrence discussed in the last chapter. Apparently the judge leant
towards deterrence and reasoned that workers were responsible
for their own safety. This left him to choose between option (3), in
these circumstances the most logical answer, or (2) a simple "but
for" test which cuts the inquiry short. Another judge on another
occasion might have selected option (1) on the ground that, given
the hazardous nature of the activity, safety belts must not only be
available on the site but also the employer must ensure that they
were worn; a "non-delegable duty of care" was owed to employees. What we are seeing is that the notion of causation is inherently subjective and capable of manipulation to fit the viewpoint
of the judge, who is left with a great deal of discretion. This is one
reason why judges opt for the compromise option in (4) of contributory negligence. In reality, this option too leaves much room
for subjective evaluation. A judge who sees industrial safety as
largely the responsibility of employers might allocate 80 per cent
of the blame to the employer and only 20 per cent to the steeplejack, a skilled worker, who ought to take a share of the responsibility; a judge who took a more robust view of the employee's
responsibility to look after himself would probably reverse these
percentages.

REMOTENESS OF DAMAGE

It has to be said that the various tests used from time to time to
mark the cut-off point for liability are quite as unreliable as the
"but for" test of causation, with which they may in any event
often be interchangeable. Currently, courts rely heavily on the
twin concepts of *foreseeability* and *remoteness*, but for many years
the standard test of liability for damage in the tort of negligence
was that of *directness*. This test was expounded in the case of *Re
Polemis* (1921), where a plank dropped into the hold of a ship by
a careless worker during unloading unexpectedly set light to
petrol vapour, causing an explosion. If we were to apply the "but
for" test to these facts, the answer would be ambiguous: "but for"
the dropping of the plank, the fire would not have occurred; alternatively, "but for" the petrol vapour, the fire would not have
occurred. In fact, the charterers were held liable for their worker's
negligence to the full extent of the damage caused; as the fire had

been "directly caused" by the negligent act, the court reasoned, the fact that it could not have been "reasonably anticipated" was immaterial. The directness test operated so as to hold the defendant liable for *all the damage that flowed directly* from the wrongful act—a rather expensive answer (Davies, 1981)!

In *Wagon Mound No 1* (1961), a very similar question came before the Privy Council. The crew of the *Wagon Mound* was responsible for an oil spillage into the waters of Sydney Harbour. Workers on nearby docks were using oxyacetylene welding equipment, sparks from which somewhat unexpectedly caused a piece of cotton waste to flare up and set light to the oil. The consequence was a mammoth fire. Applying the direct test of *Re Polemis*, the trial judge held the charterers of the *Wagon Mound* liable. Unexpectedly, the Privy Council changed course, preferring the test that only *reasonably foreseeable* damage would give rise to liability. In language reminiscent of Oliver Wendell Holmes (see above, p.30), Viscount Simonds argued for the "reasonable man" test to be applied, on the ground that:

"If it is asked why a man should be responsible for the natural or necessary or probable consequences of his act . . . the answer is not because they are natural or necessary or probable, but because, since they have this quality, it is judged, by the standard of the reasonable man, that he ought to have foreseen them . . . if some limitation must be imposed on the consequences for which the negligent actor is to be held responsible—and all are agreed that some limitation there must be—why should that test be rejected which, since he is judged by what the reasonable man ought to foresee, corresponds with the common conscience of mankind."

Wagon Mound No 2 (1967) extended the new foreseeability test to nuisance; today it is the standard test for resolving questions of remoteness throughout the law of tort.

Shortly after *Wagon Mound*, the House of Lords had to consider a case where Post Office workers had left an open manhole in the road, covered by a small tent and with paraffin lamps around the site (*Hughes v Lord Advocate*, 1963). Allured by the scene, two small boys went to play in the tent and inadvertently knocked one of the lamps into the manhole, causing a violent explosion. One of the boys suffered horrible burns. The Post Office was exonerated from liability by the trial judge, applying the *Wagon Mound* test that the damage was not foreseeable. On appeal to the

House of Lords, Lord Reid, who had shortly before been instrumental in instituting the foreseeability test, dealt brusquely with this argument. The injuries were from burns and it could not be said that injuries from burns were unforeseeable; the extent of the burns was perhaps unexpected but "damage of the same type" could have been foreseen, hence reparation would be granted for the terrible injuries.

Would it have been simpler to say that the damage flowed "directly" from the defendant's actions, bringing the wheel full circle back to *Re Polemis*? Which of the two tests is fairer varies from case to case. The "direct" test is more closely linked to causation but it can be harsh to defendants, making them liable for unexpected consequences of apparently trivial acts of negligence; the alternative test of foreseeability, which in principle relieves the defendant of responsibility for all the damage that could not have been foreseen by the reasonable man, may have equally unjust consequences. In *Lamb v Camden LBC* (1961), contractors employed by the local authority to replace a sewer negligently fractured the water main, damaging the foundations of the claimant's house. Putting her furniture in store, she went abroad, leaving the house empty. Squatters moved in, causing extensive damage. Arguably, the "but for" test is satisfied: but for the flooding the claimant would have stayed home. Arguably, the chain of events is at least as likely as what occurred in Sydney Harbour. Yet, acting largely on instinct, the Court of Appeal held the damage, even if foreseeable, too remote to claim. In *Reeves v Metropolitan Police Commissioner* (1999), by way of contrast, the liability of the police for the suicide of a man detained in custody on charges of credit fraud was in issue. The police had information of previous suicide attempts. The House of Lords had to decide whether the claimant's own deliberate act was a "new intervening act" that broke the chain of causation. Perhaps surprisingly, they held that suicide was "not outwith the contemplated scope of events to which the duty of care was directed". In other words, the injury was foreseeable even if not direct; the foreseeability test can on occasion be wider than the test of directness.

The truth is that causation and remoteness tests are all equally capable of manipulation by sympathetic judges anxious to avoid a harsh outcome. They represent only a "gut feeling" that cut-off point has been reached and cannot withstand hard logical scrutiny. The real question is one of policy: is it "fair, just and reasonable" for the police to be held responsible in these circumstances? It may be that the duty of care, conceded in the *Reeves* case, is really a better regulator. Do the police owe a duty of care to protect a vulnerable member of the public against himself? If so, what ought the extent of their duty to be?

TRAUMA AND PSYCHIATRIC INJURY

Nervous shock usually figures in textbooks as a "special problem" of duty of care. It may be hard for the modern reader to understand why it should be a problem at all. The terms "trauma", "traumatic injury", "psychiatric illness" and "mental illness" are today well understood and accepted as recognised branches of medical practice. They exist. They can be treated. They should therefore be compensated like any other injury. The problems posed by nervous shock, a term redolent of Victorian feminine weakness and suggesting a certain scepticism about its very existence, owe much to tort law's historical origins, which it has found difficulty in discarding.

The reasons why nervous shock poses problems for tort law are epitomised in the early case of *Bourhill v Young* (1942). A young woman alighting from a bus witnessed a gory traffic accident. She suffered a miscarriage and brought an action against the negligent driver claiming damages for nervous shock. It is true that some of the Law Lords did analyse the problem in terms of duty of care, reasoning that the particular claimant was insufficiently proximate because she was outside the area in which she might have suffered physical injury. This reasoning seems to suggest that psychiatric and physical injury differ in character. A different line of reasoning treats the damage as too remote, either because psychiatric injury to bystanders is not a foreseeable consequence of careless driving or perhaps because the Law Lords were not prepared to accept that fright could cause a miscarriage. In other words, there is a triangular relationship between duty of care, remoteness and causation, making nervous shock a general problem for tort law rather than merely a problem of duty. Underlying the legal analysis lie deeper practical problems. Nervous shock, the courts feel, is easily counterfeited and may produce a number of bogus claims. Once recognised, nervous injury may extend indefinitely: from those who are also physically injured; to bystanders present at an accident but not physically injured; to large numbers of people who experience traumatic events purely tangentially, like spectators round the world who witnessed the horrific events at the World Trade Centre on September 11, 2001 on television. Even if their claims are genuine, there may simply be too many. Like economic loss, the concept of psychiatric injury introduces the spectre of liability to "an indeterminate class of persons for indeterminate sums". This is a problem of remoteness of damage rather than duty.

Faced with these problems, the courts preferred to move cautiously from a relatively negative base. They have set in place a number of restrictive tests, such as the rule that a claimant must be closely related to the primary victim of the accident or must have viewed the accident with "their own unaided senses" (*McLoughlin v O'Brian*, 1982). These tests allowed courts to exercise tight control over the development of liability in this area, barring the way to a flood of actions, many of them trivial. The consequence is, however, a confusing and contradictory case law. Based on no very rational principle, it is proving difficult to rationalise or dismantle.

The problems of nervous shock and the inability of the courts to deal with them came to a head after the tragic disaster during a football match at Hillsborough stadium, when the police failed to exercise adequate crowd control and a barrier collapsed, killing and injuring a large number of spectators. (This catastrophe was mentioned in Ch.2, in the context of accountability.) Although claims for death and personal injury were settled by the police, several actions came to court, including a class action by relatives claiming damages for nervous shock (*Alcock v Chief Constable of South Yorkshire*, 1991). The claimants were closely related to those killed or injured and some of them had been present at the ground, though not within the area of physical injury. In these circumstances, the existing classifications, built up incrementally, produced some strange results: "ties of love and affection" covered death of a son or fiancé but not a brother or brother-in-law, unless a specially close-knit family could be shown. Worse was to follow, when a number of police officers on duty at the Hillsborough stadium claimed for "debilitating psychiatric harm" caused by the suffering and carnage they viewed during the aftermath of the accident (*Frost (White) v Chief Constable of South Yorkshire*, 1999). Their claim succeeded partly because they were classified as rescuers and partly because of the high duty of care that rests on employers. Faced with this serious disparity, unacceptable to public opinion, the House of Lords devised a new classification, dividing victims into two classes: "primary" victims, or those involved in the accident, were in principle eligible for damages; "secondary victims", who view horrific events on the television screen or simply hear about them, were not.

The pieces of the puzzle had been marginally rearranged. Unfortunately, however, there was no real agreement among the Law Lords as to where the cut-off point was to come: Did the class of "secondary victims" include only those directly involved in an accident or did it extend at least to those "well within the range of foreseeable physical injury"?

Ploughing further through the thicket of tangled and inconsistent case law will not help in clarification. In this area, incrementalism has gone too far and radical surgery is necessary. In England, the Law Commission has recently published a very full report (Law Com.249, 1998). Arguably, however, this stays relatively close to the existing law: it does not, for example, recommend abandoning the criterion of close ties of love and affection altogether; instead it recommends a fixed statutory list, similar to that established by the Fatal Accidents Acts, of those secondary victims entitled to recover damages for nervous shock on grounds of relationship with the primary victim. A choice will soon have to be made between two extreme but logical positions: on the one hand, total abolition of the various inadequate criteria introduced from to time by courts to limit recovery (Mullany and Handford, 1993); on the other, the equally radical suggestion that all claims for nervous shock by peripheral parties be abolished (Stapleton, 1994). There is no rational intermediate position!

PROBLEMS OF PROOF

A further problem for courts lies in the fact that the "reasonable foresight" and "fair, just and reasonable" tests come from the era of "the man on the Clapham omnibus" but have survived into the space age. They provide commonsense answers in terms of fairness (and sometimes rough justice). They are not and were not intended to be scientific. But no one would wish a space rocket to be under the control of a bus driver; the skills involved are simply not commensurate.

As science advances and medicine becomes more scientific, "ordinary man" tests are out of line. They seem simplistic, suggesting that courts do not have the tools to interpret complex statistical and scientific evidence. Yet in the current state of scientific knowledge, cause and effect cannot always be conclusively proved. Take the topical and controversial issue of tobacco. We now know it to be a dangerous substance. There is much evidence of a causal link between smoking and lung cancer. This does not mean that every case of lung cancer is caused by smoking; lung cancer has other causes. Whether or not a particular case of lung cancer results from smoking is often no more than a guess. A typical twentieth-century worker has lived in a parental home permeated by tobacco smoke, travelled to work on smoke-filled trains and worked in a smoky environment. If she goes on to develop lung cancer, which of these exposures is the "cause in fact" of her illness? Or is there some other factor that no one knows about?

These causation questions have recently arisen in asbestos cases. In *Margereson and Hancock v J.W. Roberts Ltd* (1997), the claimants, who for 30 years had lived close to asbestos manufacturers, claimed this was the cause of mesothelioma, ultimately a terminal disease. We know that only asbestos fibre causes mesothelioma. We also know that each exposure to asbestos increases the risk of mesothelioma but that the progress of the disease is not cumulative and does not worsen with multiple exposure. The judge found that no causal link between residence and mesothelioma had been recognised, although a local epidemiological survey showed 26 per cent of surveyed cases linked to the defendants' factory, some of which involved residents living close to the factory. If inside the factory asbestos dust was known to be notoriously dangerous, the judge ruled, it must be reasonably foreseeable that it remained dangerous outside (Steele and Wikeley, 1997). A bold decision!

The leading case of *Fairchild v Glenhaven Funeral Services* (2002) was more complex. The claimants had been required to work with asbestos on more than one occasion but could not show which exposure had caused their mesothelioma. Rather like the victims of the shooting party, they could not satisfy the "but for" test. They argued in the House of Lords that all they need show was that, on the balance of probabilities, the defendants had "made a material contribution" to the risk of injury. Somewhat surprisingly, this argument succeeded. The outcome was harsh. Surely this was a case for apportionment, with the defendants asked to *contribute* to the damages (Stapleton, 2002)?

The foundation for much of this compassionate case law lies with the "rogue case" of *McGhee v National Coal Board* (1973). Mr McGhee worked in a brick kiln and the dust stuck to him, not enough in itself to amount to a breach of duty of care. His employers provided no washing facilities, so that he had to cycle home covered in dust. He later developed a skin disorder, which his doctors were prepared to say was attributable to brick dust

and, although they could not say precisely how it had been contracted, they surmised that the absence of washing facilities was
at least a contributing factor. "But for" the absence of washing
facilities, the Lords effectively reasoned, the claimant would not
now have dermatitis; this was, of course, precisely what the
claimant could not prove. Just how the House of Lords reasoned
themselves to their conclusion that the claimant could succeed
has never entirely been unravelled, but so they did. As another
judge was later to say, the House of Lords took "a robust and
pragmatic approach" to the facts, drawing the "legitimate inference of fact that the defendant's negligence had materially contributed to the [claimant's] injury". What the House of Lords had
done was effectively to change the burden of proof, a change
implicitly admitted by Lord Wilberforce, who said that, "where a
person has, by breach of a duty of care, created a risk, and injury
occurs within the area of that risk, the loss should be borne by
him unless he shows that it has some other cause". In all probability they did so because—as Lord Wilberforce openly admitted—they thought it fairer for the employer, who had created the
risk and took the profits, to bear the burden of the "inherent evi-
dential difficulty" than for the risk to fall on the innocent victim.
The ambiguous language of causation veiled the change, leaving
a problem for future courts to disentangle.

The point arose again in a set of problematical medical cases,
involving complex statistical evidence, difficult to interpret. In
Wilsher v Essex AHA (1988), a child who had been born prema-
turely and placed in intensive care suffered damage from an
excess of oxygen in his blood, resulting in partial blindness. The
medical evidence was at best equivocal: on the one hand, it suggested that blindness might have resulted from an excess of oxygen due to a negligently inserted catheter; on the other hand,
statistical evidence showed that blindness often occurs in prema-
ture babies to whom oxygen has not been administered. By a
majority, the "robust" Court of Appeal ruled in favour of giving
the claimant the benefit of the doubt, a line of approach supported
by *McGhee*. This sympathetic ruling was set aside by the House of
Lords, who thought it impossible to tell from the evidence
whether or not excess oxygen was the cause of blindness. In these
circumstances, the claimant could not be said to have proved the
case on a balance of probabilities and a retrial would be necessary.
Lord Bridge referred to the danger of making the forensic process
"still more unpredictable and hazardous by distorting the law to
accommodate the exigencies of what may seem hard cases".

In terms of causation, these two cases are difficult to interpret and even harder to square with one another. The non-lawyer, however, would probably find the fuss incomprehensible. The issue is surely simple: Who is to win what we might call a "half-proved case", where the evidence is suggestive but ambiguous? The answer is, as we know, that the general burden of proof falls on the claimant. In *McGhee*, the burden of proof is lightened or very nearly reversed; in *Wilsher*, the traditional position is restored.

How can the conflicting decisions be squared? One way to resolve the medical negligence cases is by tying statistical evidence to the idea of "loss of a chance" (Lunney, 1995; Reece, 1995). Statistics tell us that a baby has a one in five chance of avoiding blindness through oxygen in the blood; the admittedly negligent act of the doctors in inserting the catheter thus deprived the *Wilsher* baby of a one in five chance. In *Hotson v East Berkshire AHA* (1987), undue delay in diagnosis of a traumatic fracture led to delay in providing adequate and appropriate treatment so that the patient suffered permanent disability. The trial judge awarded damages on the basis of statistical evidence that there was a 75 per cent risk of permanent disability and only a 25 per cent chance of full recovery; the claimant had thus lost a 25 per cent chance of recovery. (The House of Lords reinstated the traditional rule of proof on a balance of probabilities, holding that causation had not been established.)

Alternatively, the two lines of cases could be separated:

- In cases invoking employers' liability for complex industrial manufacturing processes, where the employer benefits from the worker's labour and is increasingly responsible for his health and safety, it is fair to lighten the claimant's burden of proof as a move towards enterprise liability. The added financial burden on employers can be spread through insurance and will ultimately rest on consumers.

- Where medical personnel and hospitals engaged in operations of great difficulty are involved, the issues may be different. Costs cannot be spread in the same way and courts have to be mindful of the effect of a negligence finding on the reputation of hard-pressed hospitals and medical staff.

This would still leave hard cases. In *Margereson and Hancock*, for example, courts would still have to decide whether to add near neighbours to the category of employers' liability or whether to open a new category of liability for environmental harm, a very problematic area, as we shall see in the next chapter.

RATIONALISATION?

The House of Lords was blamed for drawing back in *McGhee* from open discussion of the policy issues. In *Wilsher*, it was accused of resorting to legal fiction and linguistic ambiguity in order to obscure the radical result in *McGhee*. It may be that courts would do better to discuss the issues more openly, as Lord Steyn did for nervous shock in *Frost*. There he asserted that courts had systematically ducked the hardest questions: Whether tort law should attempt to provide redress for psychiatric injury at all and, if so, when? Deakin, Johnston and Markesinis (2003, p.82) make a similar point when they argue that some of the most difficult questions of causation and remoteness would be more easily answered by directly attacking the hard questions of what damage tort law should redress: should speculative damage, such as "loss of a chance", be claimable, for example?

The sheer complexity of modern causation actions shows how far negligence has moved from its origins in the reasonable behaviour of the reasonable man: as suggested earlier, from the Clapham omnibus to the space rocket era. Perhaps there is something to be said for a return in that direction, with negligence governed by the simple question, "Is it in all the circumstances fair, just and reasonable for the defendant to compensate this claimant?" This would reflect the part played by civil juries in the United States. Nervous shock could then be simply one form of personal injury, as Mullany and Handford advocate. Damages would be the subject of a negotiated settlement, based on the concepts of contribution and apportionment advocated by Stapleton (2002, p.26). But moves to contribution and apportionment cross Lord Pearson's principle/policy boundary: both "raise difficult questions of policy, as well as involving the introduction of new legal principles rather than extension of some principle already recognized and operating". These issues are unsuited for the incremental methods of judicial process. They would expose the judiciary to charges of lawmaking and judicial activism. Someone else must intervene.

FURTHER READING

See generally Stapleton's chapter, "Unpacking Causation", in *Relating to Responsibility* (Cane and Gardner ed., Oxford, Hart Publishing, 2001). There is no substitute for struggling with the difficult nervous shock cases, contained in Hepple, Howarth and Matthews at 118–129; there are numerous other references in this comprehensive text. The issue of nervous shock are discussed by Teff, "Liability for Psychiatric Illness: Advancing Cautiously" (1992) 12 *Oxford Journal of Legal Studies*, a note on the Law Commission report on psychiatric damage. Lunney discusses "loss of chance" as a head of damage in "What Price A Chance?" (1995) 15 *Legal Studies* 1. The significant case of *Fairchild v Glenhaven Funeral Services* has been noted by Morgan, "Lost Causes in the House of Lords: *Fairchild v Glenhaven Funeral Services*" (2003) 66 *Modern Law Review* 277 and Stapleton, "Lords A'Leaping Evidentiary Gaps" (2002) 10 *Torts Law Journal* 376.

5

LAND USE AND TORT LAW

QUIET ENJOYMENT

For centuries agriculture was the main rural activity and the ownership of land was an important status symbol. This was an inheritance from the feudal society where land tenure underlay the political system in which our common law originated. It is not therefore very surprising that the common law strongly protected interests in land: Blackstone (1787, p.167) listed six causes of action relating directly to real property. *Trespass to land* is a nominate tort of great antiquity, originally designed to secure to the landowner possession and enjoyment of his land, interests in land also protected by the ancient nominate tort of *nuisance*. Historically, both could be used to decide disputes about ownership and possession of property and typically came to court when one person had tried to dispossess another of his land (Fifoot, 1949, p.3). In this respect, the common law differs from systems based on Roman law, where title to land and property form part of the law of real and personal property and not of the law of delict. The common law was firmly on the side of the owner or occupier of land, who was entitled to deter trespassers, often in practice poachers, by violent and sometimes barbaric means. Today, when farming has become agribusiness and tourism runs it close as the major rural industry, the countryside is increasingly a playground for the cities. Far from authorising the use of mantraps, Parliament has recently introduced "right to roam" legislation in the Countryside and Rights of Way Act 2000, which opens up private property to ramblers, justifying what would otherwise be trespass.

The drift to the towns started by the Industrial Revolution means, however, that most people today live in increasingly crowded and polluted urban surroundings. There is heavy pressure on land use. Ownership has greatly expanded, with a high percentage of the population now owning their own homes. Landowners are no longer free to use their property for their own purposes, subject only to controls imposed by the common law, particularly through the tort of nuisance. For nearly a century, planning legislation has regulated in great detail the use to which private owners can put their land. Statute has also created a large number of trivial regulatory offences to outlaw minor nuisances, such a noisy neighbours or high hedges, turning them into public nuisances and rendering it possible for local authorities to take action against the perpetrators. Statute also provides for the compulsory acquisition of land for public purposes, ranging from public housing and the supply of gas, electricity and water, through roads and international airports to nuclear installations. Nuisance in the shape of noise and pollution caused by these developments to adjacent landowners may also be authorised by statute.

We are beginning to realise the extent to which our lifestyle is irreversibly changing the nature of the countryside, and ecological and environmental issues are consequently progressing steadily up the political agenda. Responsibility for environmental issues has moved upwards to international and transnational bodies, all of which promulgate treaties, conventions and directives on matters ranging from agricultural subsidies to control of habitat, pollution and waste disposal, that tie the hands of national governments and courts. For the United Kingdom, the European Union is the most important body, as its policies result in law binding on the UK and limiting government options. The EU has, for example, regulated the critical areas of water quality and waste disposal, both central to the tort of nuisance. It has also added a substantial environmental dimension to the procedural requirements of major development projects, such as roads or airports, all of which now need a detailed environmental impact assessment before planning permission can be granted.

Our environment has, in short, changed very greatly in a very short time. In this chapter, we shall be asking whether the lines drawn by the common law around the use and enjoyment of land are drawn in the right place to accommodate these changes. We shall be looking at new uses for the old torts of trespass and nuisance, and considering the why the courts are so unwilling to expand them. We shall also be asking whether the tort of nuisance can usefully be adapted to a post-modern, post-industrialised society, in which an ever greater percentage of the population lives and works in big cities.

THE USES OF TRESPASS TO LAND

Trespass to land, which consists of intentionally entering, remaining on, or placing any object on someone else's land without consent, is technically a tort of strict liability. By this we mean only that the tort is actionable without proof of damage; in other words, merely to enter someone's land is actionable. We must not read too much into the word "intentional". It implies that the trespasser must be on the land of his own volition but it does *not* imply a wrongful motive or culpability. This point is vividly illustrated by an old case in which a police constable, seeing a door open at night, entered a barn to check that no crime had been committed and was injured when he fell into an open pit. He failed in a claim against the occupier on the ground that he was technically a trespasser, an unfair outcome that one hopes might be affected by the Occupiers Liability Act 1984 (see above, p.19).

Compared with the volume of personal injuries litigation discussed in earlier chapters, trespass to land is merely a footnote to the real business of tort law. But trespass actions are still systematically used by the Ramblers' Association to challenge blocked access to footpaths and public rights of way of way across land, and the RA also defends ramblers who are challenged as trespassers. Again, during the 1970s, when it was fashionable for "squatters" to take over empty property in protest against housing shortages, the trespass action was used to evict them. The tort has also been used as a weapon in the bitter and often violent campaign against hunting. The League Against Cruel Sports, for example, once brought a celebrated test case against the Master of a Hunt, who was held liable for trespass when the hunt followed a stag on to the property of a farmer opposed to stag hunting (*League Against Cruel Sports Ltd v Scott*, 1986). This technique can be turned against hunt protesters or anti-vivisectionists if they trespass on private property during their campaigning activities. In the case of animal rights activists and anti-vivisectionists, it may indeed be a significant weapon, as these campaigning groups often do a great deal of wilful and deliberate damage, letting animals out of cages and setting fire to premises, adding up to much more than a nominal trespass.

Other cases draw on tort law to construct a right to privacy, as we have seen, not generally protected by English law. In *Harrison v Duke of Rutland* (1893), someone "passed and repassed" on a road running through private land with the motive of disrupting a grouse shoot, while in *Hickman v Maisey* (1900), a snooper stood on the highway in order to spy on racehorses in training on neighbouring land; both were held to be trespassing on the highway. Asked what interest tort law was protecting in these cases, the reader would probably reply "privacy". Yet in *Bernstein v Skyviews* (1987), where the defendants took an aerial photograph of B's house for commercial purposes, the judge refused to extend the tort of trespass to encompass air space over the claimant's land.

More typically, trespass and nuisance actions are used in seemingly trivial cases in district courts to settle disputes between neighbouring property-owners over boundary fences and party walls. Courts have at their disposal the powerful weapon of an injunction to stop trespass or bring nuisances to an end. A trespassing neighbour can be ordered to move a boundary fence or party wall or an order made to reopen a closed footpath or restore it if it has been ploughed. Keeping noisy birds or smelly pigs can be prohibited. In seemingly trivial cases, passions often run surprisingly high. When neighbours recently quarrelled over a crowing cockerel, for example, the loving owner spent £30,000 on trying to establish her right to keep the bird, only abandoning the fight on the point of bankruptcy. Using the threat of an injunction, a judge may be in a position to negotiate a sensible compromise. The ringing of church bells might, for instance, be permitted only for limited periods and at reasonable hours. Injunctions can be granted to stop building works during the evening to allow local residents to get some sleep and recreation. Noisy clubs can be closed down after midnight (this is a public nuisance, which allows the local authority to take action). The situation becomes more delicate where the court feels that, although a legal right has been infringed, an injunction to bring the activity to a halt is not in the best interests of the community. Since 1858, courts have had the power to substitute an award of damages for an injunction whenever this seems appropriate. In practice, however, they seem unwilling to do this. In *Miller v Jackson* (1977), use of the village green as a cricket club caused annoyance after a housing estate had been constructed. Balls were several times hit into the garden of the nearest house, frightening the householder, damaging plants and breaking glass. The Court of Appeal found this to be a nuisance but refused an injunction. The only judge prepared to go so far wanted the order suspended to allow time to find a new pitch. This is an area of considerable judicial discretion, where some judges clearly feel that private rights ought not to be subordinated to a supposed public interest and that damages amounting to a compulsory purchase order of the landowner's rights ought not to be allowed without proper statutory backing.

Still more delicate and controversial is the use of trespass in conjunction with public and private nuisance as "public order torts", against demonstrators, strikers and pickets. Trespass was used in this way to expel miners from National Coal Board property during the 1985 miners' strike and also against the "Greenham women", who cut the wire (trespass to goods) and entered United States air force bases (trespass to land) to protest against the use of nuclear missiles. Many of these cases entail use of the public highway by demonstrators. This may involve three torts: trespass to the highway, private nuisance if there is more than trivial annoyance to neighbouring landowners, and the closely related tort of public nuisance, which always involves a minor criminal offence, in this case obstruction of the highway, an offence under the Highways Act 1980. To sit-in or demonstrate *on* private property is a trespass; demonstrations *outside* premises may amount to all three torts. In *Hubbard v Pitt* (1976), for example, demonstrators objecting to the discriminatory racial practices of a local estate agent picketed the premises with placards. Even this entirely orderly and peaceful protest was held to constitute a nuisance, on the ground that the regular picketing interfered with the owners' use and enjoyment of their premises, harming their business. In *Thomas v National Union of Mineworkers* (1986), the picketing was admittedly much less peaceful, as the affair took place in the context of a bitter national dispute over the future of the coalmining industry in which the true opponents were government and unions. At one point in the case, Scott J. robustly maintained that any unreasonable interference with the rights of others was actionable in tort and, more specifically, that interference with an individual's lawful use of the highway was either a public or a private nuisance.

There were large-scale demonstrations against new roads programmes at Twyford Down in 1993–94, on the ground that, unnecessarily and in defiance of EC requirements for an environmental impact assessment, grave ecological harm was being caused to a site of special scientific interest. A new twist was given to the civil law when it was used against the protesters by the *contractors* to threaten actions in trespass and conspiracy to recover £1.9 million allegedly caused in economic loss through the demonstrations.

Not only is there considerable overlap in this area between torts but criminal and civil law also overlap: for strikes and demonstrations, there could be criminal charges of conspiracy or charges under the Public Order Act 1986. This legislation followed widespread and largely hostile media coverage of the violent tactics used by anti-hunting campaigners and the Animal Liberation Front, which came together with front page coverage of the difficulties experienced by local farmers in expelling "New Age Travellers" from private land: the civil law procedures were too slow, too costly, etc. *DPP v Jones* (1999), a criminal case of great constitutional importance, illustrates the overlap between civil and criminal law and between the various torts and also shows why these cases are highly controversial and arouse great passions. The defendants, who were protesting against refusal to open Stonehenge to the public for druidic ceremonies on the night of the midsummer solstice, had been arrested when standing peacefully on the grass verge of the highway in contravention of a police order in terms of the Public Order Act 1986. In deciding whether the order was lawful, the House of Lords had to come to a decision on what were the limits of public access to the highway, stated in earlier case law to be strictly limited to a right of "passing and repassing": in other words, the highway is for travel and travel alone. Significantly, given the political implications, the House of Lords could not agree over the extent of the public right to use the highway, although a majority felt that it did need adjusting. Lord Irvine, then Lord Chancellor and recently responsible for introducing the Human Rights Act, boldly argued for a public right of peaceful assembly on the highway provided the "primary right of the public to pass and repass the highway was not obstructed". Lords Clyde and Lord Hutton were prepared to say that to hold a peaceful public assembly on the highway was not always unlawful. Dissenting, Lords Slynn and Hope thought that extension could be only as far as "reasonably incidental uses associated with passage". This leaves the civil law rights of landowners affected by demonstrators and trespassers in some confusion. By and large, judges have favoured landowners; in the light of the added protection given to the right of association by the Human Rights Act 1998, which domesticates ECHR Art.11, the law may, as Lord Irvine asserted, need rebalancing.

THE BOUNDARIES OF NUISANCE

A brief working definition of nuisance is that it is an annoyance that interferes indirectly with the use and enjoyment of land by its owner or occupier. Nuisance is a more complex tort than trespass and one which judges as well as students find elusive. Professor Newark, in a seminal article frequently relied on by the judiciary, describes it as "the least satisfactory department" of tort law (though the present author can think of others). Newark attributes the uncertain boundaries of the subject to "its mongrel origins". By this he means that the tort that today is called nuisance is really a bundle of torts or separate causes of action, which over the centuries have become mixed up with each other despite the fact that they do not necessarily share the same characteristics (Newark, 1949).

Newark's picture of a "bundle of torts" goes some way to explain why the tort that we today call public nuisance does not conform to our brief working definition. To sue in public nuisance one does not necessarily need to own or occupy land while, in sharp contrast to private nuisance, actions for personal injury sometimes succeed provided the other criteria for public nuisance are fulfilled. So what precisely is a public nuisance? The irritating answer is that no precise definition can be given. Fortunately, we do not need to know the answer; it is sufficient to note the elements. For our purposes, a public nuisance is:

- a state of affairs that annoys or obstructs

- a section of the public; and

- constitutes a minor criminal offence; and

- causes "special damage" to a given individual.

The subject matter of the two torts of public and private nuisance has much in common and, as we have already seen, they frequently overlap. Many public nuisances involve forms of pollution prohibited at common law, such as the pollution of water supplies, an ancient common law wrong, or the emission of noxious fumes or noise. Many of these are now collected and criminalised by the Environmental Protection Act 1990. As already indicated, obstruction of the highway is a public nuisance when it prevents the public from "passing and repassing", actionable by any individual who has suffered "special damage". In *Hubbard*, for example, the firm's private interest in the use of its business premises was inhibited by the demonstration but there was also obstruction of the sidewalk, a public nuisance from which the firm suffered special damage. Again, in *Thomas*, Scott J.

granted an injunction on the ground that interference with another's right to use the highway was a "species of private nuisance" but he also thought that the label hardly mattered. Many other modern cases reveal confusion between several of Newark's "bundle of torts".

The first point to remember about the tort that today we call *private nuisance* is that it protects the rights of a landowner to the use and enjoyment of his land. This classification can be subdivided: some of the rights, such as the right to draw water, fish or cultivate the soil, are physical in character and might also be described as "natural". Others are less tangible: for example, the right to a pleasant outlook or peace and quiet. This second type of right could be loosely classified under the head of "amenity". In practice, the two categories overlap, causing confusion: noxious fumes from a factory chimney may, for example, erode the stonework of buildings but, by making a home less pleasant to live in, they also diminish amenity. Enter a complication, introduced in the mid-nineteenth century. Like trespass, nuisance had developed in an agricultural society as a tort of strict liability. Its use was predominantly rural. Its realm was:

"The stinking privy, the urban hog-sty, the fouled or diverted stream, the polluting chimney . . . the pack of hounds next door which barked all night; it also protected against the ill effects of the neighbour's attempt to use and develop his property as he saw fit. It drew the line around free use and enjoyment of land at that point where another's use and enjoyment were impaired, and the standards for judging impairment were rural, agricultural, and conservative." (Brenner, 1973, pp.403–404).

Some of these colourful examples can be prolonged into modern life: to pollute a river with industrial waste or agricultural slurry, preventing the riparian owners from fishing; to operate a sewage farm so that it overflows on to a housing estate; to allow the fumes from a factory to blight the countryside; all these are, we shall see, the stuff of nuisance actions. But after the Industrial Revolution, land use had changed very rapidly. If landowners were entitled to protect the rural uses and amenities of their land through a tort of strict liability, progress, and particularly industrial progress, could be brought to a standstill. If land is not perpetually to be dedicated to rural use, with all other uses either prohibited or to be purchased at the going rate of damages, judges have to walk carefully in protecting amenity. This was the problem that faced the House of Lords in the leading case of *St Helens Smelting Co v Tipping* (1865).

Mr Tipping was, somewhat ironically, a mill owner who had bought an estate on the outskirts of St Helens only to find it polluted by the industrial processes of the very factories that had contributed to his own great fortune. The "noxious vapours" exhaled by the St Helens smelting works were capable of stripping foliage from trees and shrubs and blasting the crops; indeed, social historians tell us that the position had become so severe in the North of England that it was rare to see a tree in an industrial area with a single leaf, even in midsummer. Although they do not say so, the House of Lords must have known this since, three years earlier, a Select Committee of the House had published an exhaustive report into industrial pollution and the inefficacy of the common law in dealing with the matter. In any event, the House held the emissions to be a nuisance for which the company was strictly liable. In this celebrated passage from the judgment of the Lord Chancellor, Lord Westbury, he explains why the action succeeded:

"My Lords, in matters of this description it appears to me that it is a very desirable thing to mark the difference between an action brought for a nuisance upon the ground that the alleged nuisance produces material injury to the property, and an action brought for a nuisance on the ground that the thing alleged to be a nuisance is productive of sensible personal discomfort. With regard to the latter, namely, the personal inconvenience and interference with one's enjoyment, one's quiet, one's personal freedom, anything that discomposes or injuriously affects the senses or the nerves, whether that may or may not be demonstrated as nuisance, must undoubtedly depend greatly on the circumstances of the place where the thing complained of actually occurs. If a man lives in a town, it is necessary that he should subject himself to the consequences of those operations of trade which may be carried on in his immediate locality, which are actually necessary for trade and commerce, and also for the enjoyment of property, and for the benefit of the inhabitants of the town and of the public at large. If a man lives in a street where there are numerous shops, and a shop is opened next door to him, which is carried on in a fair and reasonable way, he has no ground for complaint, because to himself individually there may arise much discomfort from the trade carried on in that shop. But when an occupation is carried on by one person in the neighbourhood of another, and the result of that trade, or occupation, or business, is a material injury to property, then there unquestionably arises a very different consideration. I think, my Lords, that in a case of that description, the submission which is required from persons living in a society to that amount of discomfort which may be necessary for the legitimate and free exercise of the trade of their neighbours, would not apply to circumstances the immediate result of which is sensible injury to the value of the property."

So contrary to what we have so far been saying, we find that private nuisance is *not* always a tort of strict liability. When "material" damage to land, however trivial, is present, the liability is strict; when, as the quaint wording of the judgment puts it, the nuisance causes "sensible personal discomfort" or loss of amenity, the test is different: the court is entitled to take into consideration the expectations of the residents together with the behaviour of a "reasonable neighbour" living in the particular locality. In the well-worn Victorian formula, "What would be a nuisance in Berkeley Square would not necessarily be one in Bermondsey" (*Sturges v Bridgman*, 1879).

There are inherent problems with this classification, which may overlap confusingly. Take Mr Tipping's estate of leafless trees, blasted crops and polluted streams. It had been rendered infertile (material or physical damage). It was also unprofitable (economic loss). It was unlikely to be saleable (pure economic loss). It was certainly not an agreeable residence (loss of amenity) and it was probably also unhealthy, capable of causing physical illness (personal injuries). In the *St Helens* case, the fumes from factories caused loss of amenity, which might have resulted in symptoms such as asthma. The *St Helens* decision seemingly leaves open two potential causes of action in nuisance in respect of the same damage, one pointing to strict liability, the other to liability based on the characteristics of the neighbourhood in which the claimant resides. It also allows for overlap between negligence and nuisance in cases where "personal discomfort" and "personal injury" come together.

Once we know that nuisance is designed to protect interests in *land*, further deductions follow logically. The first is that only someone with an interest in land can use the action, a point very recently confirmed by the House of Lords in *Hunter v Canary Wharf* (see above, p.16). Secondly, the nuisance action should not cover damage other than damage to land or the use of land; nuisance should not extend to personal injuries. In *Margereson and Hancock*, for instance, the judge compared the situation of a worker and a resident living close to the factory, both of whom contracted asbestosis. It would seem unfair if the latter was better placed to win because he could sue for loss of amenity in nuisance, while the worker had to show negligence. We shall find judges in modern cases trying to eliminate remaining disparities by merging variant standards of liability: thus we find the "reasonable neighbour" of nuisance behaving in similar fashion to the "reasonable man" of negligence. These are all ways to restrain the growth of nuisance.

Before we go on to look at the modern case law, we need to consider a second fork in the branches of nuisance. In *Rylands v Fletcher* (1868), a reservoir constructed on the defendant's land by a negligent contractor burst, flooding the claimant's coalmine. The courts drew on the old precedents of strict liability in "material damage" cases of nuisance to fashion a principle of strict liability, which came to be called the rule in *Rylands v Fletcher*, giving the impression of a new nominate tort. Blackburn J., reading the judgment of the Exchequer Chamber, stated the "true rule of law" to be:

"The person who, for his own purposes, brings on his land, and collects and keeps there anything likely to do mischief if it escapes, must keep it in at his peril, and, if he does not do so, he is prima facie answerable for all the damage which is the natural consequence of its escape."

Affirming that the landowner was strictly liable for the escape of water from the reservoir, Lord Cairns, in the House of Lords, added two critical phrases (emphasis added):

"The defendants, treating them as the owners or occupiers of the close on which the reservoir was constructed, might lawfully have used that close for any purpose for which it might, *in the ordinary course of the enjoyment of land*, be used, and if, in what I may term *the natural user of that land*, there had been any accumulation of water, either on the surface or underground, and if by the operation of the laws of nature that accumulation of water had passed off into the close occupied by the plaintiff, the plaintiff could not have complained that that result had taken place."

Rylands split the area of strict liability into two nearly indistinguishable areas:

- The first derives from the earlier *St Helens* decision and is still labelled nuisance. It occurs where a state of affairs that exists on one person's land causes material damage to that of another.

- The second comes into play where something inherently dangerous "escapes" and causes damage. It has become known as the rule in *Rylands v Fletcher*. It could form the basis of an exceptional liability for hazardous activities.

The classic cases left unanswered many questions that we shall not attempt to answer, for example: What is a "thing likely to do mischief"? What is the "natural" use of land? More important, the cases show potential for clash between private property interests in a rural, landowning and conservative society and a rapidly growing industrial society, in which negligence was increasingly setting the standards.

Just as we met the argument that, in negligence, "individuals blazed the trail but enterprises reaped the profits under the protection of the law", so it has been argued that nineteenth-century judges, imbued with the prevailing laissez-faire economic philosophy of their era, deliberately tried to rid the law of the old, strict liability torts and replace them with the less severe standard of "reasonableness" in the interests of commerce and industry (Brenner, 1973). *Rylands* contains a principle quite as flexible as Lord Atkin's neighbour principle, well capable of development as a safeguard against damage caused by hazardous activity. A nineteenth-century judge, declining to adopt the precedent in the United States, explains why this has not occurred:

"We must have factories, machinery, dams, canals and railroads. If I have any of these upon my lands, and they are not a nuisance and not so managed as to become such, I am not responsible for any damage they accidentally and unavoidably do my neighbour. He receives his compensation for such damage by the general good, in which he shares." (*Losee v Buchanan*, 1873)

Whether or not Brenner is correct in his assessment of judicial opinion, in arriving at this position the courts were moving in a direction generally approved by Parliament. Development was not after all wholly in the hands of private developers nor was it carried out wholly on private property. Even before the introduction of land use planning, most large-scale development needed parliamentary authority. Roads and bridges were often financed by public subscription, and those who built them operated under statutory authority. Railways, dams and reservoirs, gasworks and power stations operated and were financed indifferently by municipal councils, private corporations or public trusts. Parliament took a hand in apportioning liability. Some of the statutes that authorised the activities of "statutory undertakers" provided specifically for civil liability, though more often they did not. Other statutes began specifically to exclude the strict liability of nuisance by inserting a "no nuisance" clause, designed specifically to bar actions in nuisance and the accompanying injunction that could bring the activities to a full stop. Statutory compensation schemes were also introduced for landowners whose land was compulsorily purchased. In *Hammersmith Railway v Brand* (1869), the House of Lords ruled by a narrow majority that such a scheme did not cover tangential loss: a statute authorising the construction of a railway necessarily authorised consequential nuisance in the form of noise and vibration from passing trains. Leaning to negligence liability, courts developed the double principle that:

- liability for nuisance is deemed to be excluded whenever a judge is satisfied that the authorised activity cannot be carried on without causing a nuisance;

- negligence liability is excluded *only* if statute expressly so provides or if sense cannot be made of the statute without this implication.

In a multiplicity of cases, the defence of "statutory authority" had become a crucial factor in restricting strict liability in nuisance; *Rylands* was to be similarly transformed. As industry developed and became the norm, the courts moved from a position in which agricultural use is the "natural user of land" and virtually every other use non-natural, to the opposite pole, where manufacturing industry is considered "natural", unless perhaps it is exceptionally hazardous. But when the manufacture of munitions was held a natural use of land in wartime (*Read v Lyons*, 1947), the rule had been emasculated. *Rylands* still figures in the textbooks and lip service is paid to it. In practice, its empire has been restricted to occasional, marginal cases, while negligence, the general principle of civil liability, covers every other situation. Strict liability has become a tiny, residual island, surrounded by an engulfing sea of fault.

In the Australian case of *Goldman v Hargrave* (1967) a gum tree struck by lightning was pulled down and sawn into sections, but left to smoulder on land that had been cleared. The tree flared up, causing a disastrous fire to rage through the Australian bush. The case for the claimants was that the defendant had created a hazardous situation; consequently, a fire had escaped, which he had failed to contain. The defence was that the hazard originated from a natural object, which was naturally on the land; neither nuisance nor *Rylands* was applicable in such a case. Complaining of the arbitrary basis of a rule that tries to distinguish "natural" and "non-natural" use of land, the Privy Council avoided *Rylands*, choosing an alternative ground for liability:

"The case is not one where a person has brought a source of danger on to his land, nor one where the occupier has so used his property as to cause a danger to his neighbour. It is one where an occupier, faced with a hazard accidentally arising on his land, fails to act with reasonable prudence so as to remove the hazard. The issue is therefore whether in such a case the occupier is guilty of legal negligence, which involves the issue whether he is under a duty of care, and, if so, what is the scope of that duty."

In *Leakey v National Trust* (1980), the English Court of Appeal adopted this Privy Council decision. The National Trust had on its land an Anglo-Saxon burial mound. Soil slipping from the mound threatened a neighbouring house. Ruling out strict liability in nuisance, the Court of Appeal also curtailed the nuisance defence that the mound was "naturally" on the soil. They fell back on a novel and unpredictable duty to do "what the particular man, not the average man, can be expected to do" to prevent damage caused by natural objects. Although the Court of Appeal denied this, one way to analyse the case is that it imposes a duty of care to prevent a state of affairs that is not a nuisance. How can the change be justified or explained? (See Markesinis, 1989.)

The simplest explanation is that the courts, without abandoning the framework of a "law of torts", are slowly moving to a law of tort, with fault as the basis of civil liability, yet loss sharing is the best solution for *Goldman*, where the losses caused by bush fires are so extreme that they are best left to lie where they fall. Or could an alternative justification be found in theories of rational loss allocation, the reasoning being that the landowner, rather than the victim, ought to bear the costs of the "enterprise" and bear the considerable burden of insurance (Ogus and Richardson, 1977)? This is the line apparently taken by the court in *Leakey's* case. Similar reasoning was used both by Pearson and the Law Commission to justify a principle of strict liability to cover "ultra-hazardous activity" (Law Com. 1970; Pearson, 1978). Criticised by academics because defining ultra-hazardous or high-risk activities is quite as problematic as identifying the "natural" use of land, the recommendations were shelved by an apathetic Parliament.

PALE GREEN TORTS?

We are now in a position to consider whether these strict liability torts, sometimes described as environmental torts, are capable of playing any role in environmental protection. Are the liability lines drawn in the right place for post-industrial society? And are the courts moving them in the right direction?

What we have seen is a set of torts designed for the protection of private property interests in a rural, agricultural and conservative society, clinging on with difficulty to survive the Industrial Revolution and enduring into an era in which environmental protection has become a political issue. In their critique of tort law, Conaghan and Mansell (1993, p.118) describe nuisance as "a pale green tort" because, although it is capable of protecting the environment and occasionally does so, this is incidental to its main aims:

"Nuisance law has never really reflected a concern for environmental protection as such. The primary focus of nuisance has been to define the rights and limitations attaching to the enjoyment of private property. Environmental damage is only relevant in so far as it poses a threat of harm to someone's proprietary interests. The wrong lies in the violation of property rights not in the destruction of the environment."

The authors suggest, in other words, that torts designed for the protection of private property interests will never be adequate tools for environmental protection.

Environmentalists tend to argue that what we are seeing in modern times is deliberate failure by the judiciary fully to utilise the torts' potential and transform them into torts of purest green. According to this view, *Cambridge Water Co v Eastern Counties Leather* (1994) is a missed opportunity to use torts of strict liability to "make the polluter pay". ECL owned a tannery, situated about 1.3 miles from the water company's borehole. Percloroethene, a solvent used in tanning, had at some time in the past seeped into the ground beneath the tannery and contaminated the supply of drinking water from the borehole. Following an EC Directive, the chemical had to be removed at some cost before the water could be supplied as drinking water. Reversing the trial judge, the Court of Appeal held ECL strictly liable in nuisance or *Rylands v Fletcher*. Applying *Wagon Mound No 2* (see above, p.61) and skilfully reinterpreting the rule in *Rylands v Fletcher*, the House of Lords unanimously overturned the Court of Appeal decision: the judge had found the chain of events to be unforeseeable and foreseeability was the test of liability for damage in both of the strict liability torts. The case can be viewed as just a further step in the onward march of negligence but that is not to say that the House of Lords was blind to the issues of environmental policy. This is what Lord Goff had to say:

"The protection and preservation of the environment is now perceived as being of crucial importance to the future of mankind; and public bodies, both national and international, are taking significant steps towards the establishment of legislation which will promote the protection of the environment, and make the polluter pay for the damage to the environment for which he is responsible . . . But it does not follow from these developments that a common law principle, such as the rule in *Rylands v Fletcher*, should be developed or rendered more strict to provide for liability in respect of such pollution. On the contrary, given that so much well-informed and carefully structured legislation is now being put in place for this purpose, there is less need for the courts to develop a common law principle to achieve the same end, and indeed it may well be undesirable that they should do so."

Arguably, the House of Lords was not being asked to *develop* common law principles but simply to *apply* them, the true development being their decision to introduce the negligence "foreseeability" test. And if it is wrong to "develop a common law principle" in this area, we might ask, what is to be said for *Leakey*, which cut out a well-established common law defence to strict liability and grafted on an uncertain negligence test (Wilkinson, 1994)?

In 1865, the *St Helens* case was a significant victory for the environment when a second application by Mr Tipping resulted in an injunction, which closed down the defendant's factory. Nearly a century later, a test case brought by landowners to fight river pollution ended with mandatory injunctions to end sewage and industrial discharges into the River Derwent and to restore depleted fishing stocks (*Pride of Derby and Derbyshire Angling Association v British Celanese Ltd and Derbyshire Corporation*, 1953). This cost the local authority £1,800,000 for a new sewage works and cost manufacturers £180,000 for an industrial electricity cooling system. But as Parliament took over responsibility for planning and planning legislation came into general operation, courts have understandably become more cautious. When residents living near the port of Milford Haven complained of nuisance caused by heavy traffic and danger occasioned by the new oil refinery, the courts were understandably hesitant. Parliament had, after all, specifically approved the zoning of Milford Haven as an important industrial port. Reasoning that the intention of Parliament must have been "to change the immediate environment of the village", the House of Lords ruled that levels of noise and air pollution were "inevitable in a neighbourhood in which oil refinery business is to be regarded as the norm" (*Allen v Gulf Oil Refining*, 1981).

In the recent *Marcic v Thames Water Utilities Ltd* (2002) litigation, Thames Water, a privatised commercial water authority, allowed sewage to escape at regular intervals into M's garden. M, who had spent a considerable sum on amelioration, requested damages for loss of amenity and for consequential diminution in the value of his property. Thames Water relied on settled case law from the nineteenth century exempting water authorities from liability in nuisance on the ground that their activities were of "general benefit to the community". The three courts faced this barrier very differently.

- The first judge was bound by the authorities. He drew on the Human Rights Act to suggest a right to compensation for violation of the right to respect for private life under ECHR Art.8.

- The Court of Appeal rejected this approach but was happy to overturn the authorities and bring the immunity to an end. Faced with arguments over cost, they thought it "at least arguable that those who make use of the sewerage system should be charged sufficient to cover the cost of paying compensation to the minority who suffer damage as a consequence of the operation of the system".

- To the House of Lords, this line of reasoning was untenable. Liability in nuisance was thought by Lord Nicholls to be wholly incompatible with the scheme of the Water Industry Act 1991, which regulated the whole industry; the antiquated rules of nuisance, designed to regulate relations between neighbouring landowners, were simply not applicable to a system designed to manage the supply of water to the community plus a countrywide system of sewage disposal. Lord Hoffmann thought capital expenditure by a statutory public utility, involved very different considerations to those raised by a bipolar relationship between two adjacent landowners; where these were in issue, it was the court's duty, whatever the difficulties, "to perform its usual function of deciding what is reasonable between the two parties", but the exercise became very different when dealing with capital expenditure of a statutory undertaking providing public utilities on a large scale:

"If one customer is given a certain level of services, everyone in the same circumstances should receive the same level of services. So the effect of a decision about what it would be reasonable to expect a sewerage undertaker to do for the plaintiff is extrapolated across the country."

The reasoning of the House of Lords in *Marcic* approaches an argument for a public law of torts (see Ch.8) but Buckley (2002, p.210), picking up the economic arguments considered in Ch.2, argues that profit-making organisations like Thames Water should be submitted "to the full rigour of private law disciplines". Although privatised, the water industry is heavily regulated and price rises need the approval of the water regulator; shortly after *Marcic*, permission was obtained for a price rise to help towards the costs of rectifying sewage spills. Buckley's argument places greater weight on the deterrent effects of tort law than they can bear (Harlow, 2004, pp.31–35).

CONCLUSIONS

The many cases discussed in this chapter present a strange contrast with those considered in Ch.3. The rule in *Donoghue* became the twentieth century's general principle of civil liability; just as clearly formulated and capable of development, the potential of the rule in *Rylands* is ignored, its scope and ambit steadily eroded. Why?

The principal reason, articulated in many of the judgments, is the desire of the judiciary to systematise the law of tort. The tort law under construction by our judges is, for historical reasons, being built on foundations of negligence. As we have seen in this chapter, the torts that protect interests in land are not for the most part based on negligence and therefore contain the potential for serious anomaly. Consider the suggestion made earlier that local residents exposed to dust by an asbestos manufacturer might be able to claim in nuisance for loss of amenity or for escape of a dangerous material under *Rylands*. This could theoretically give them rights greater than those of an employee. Then think back to the nervous shock cases discussed in Ch.4 and remember the disparity that arose in *Frost* and *Alcock* (see above, p.69). Now consider the argument that noise and vibrations result in sleep deprivation and nervous illness. This is the type of anomaly that Lord Goff does not wish to see extended by the incursion of nuisance or *Rylands* into the area of personal injuries, dominated by "the now fully developed law of negligence".

But if, as Lord Goff seems to think, nuisance is a "tort *to* land", what is the justification for failing to utilise its potential in defence of the environment? Arguably, it could be used to bring to an end a host of environmental dangers. Wind farms could be closed down on the ground of noise; genetically engineered crops could become the subject of *Rylands* actions if they "escaped" from the land; and so on. This may or may not be in the public interest. To turn nuisance into a "toxic tort", as some environmentalists certainly wish (Steele, 1995, p.236), would move courts on to dangerous ground, involving them, as in medical negligence cases, in the evaluation of difficult, contested and rapidly changing scientific evidence. Complaints of "a Luddite law of torts" could certainly be anticipated.

As Lord Goff observed in the *Cambridge Water* case, the field is heavily regulated and "well-informed and carefully structured legislation" is gradually being put in place. Policymaking has moved up to EU level. Tort law, we saw when considering deterrence, is at its least effective in redressing environmentally related injury. It is on balance more important to regulate, prohibit, control and detoxify than to provide a retrospective remedy in damages, especially where "historic pollution" through chemicals not considered toxic at the time they were used is in question, as in the *Cambridge Water* case. Tort law is a blunt instrument and a "penalty default" regulatory regime may be fairer and more effective. True, a court can award a mandatory injunction to end pollution; we saw this done in the *Pride of Derby* case with sewage and industrial discharges into the River Derwent, but we also saw in the Milford Haven case how unwilling courts are to take this action, especially where large-scale industrial development is concerned and Parliament has considered the matter or planning permission has been granted. What would the courts have thought of a request from Mr Hunter to demolish Canary Wharf? Courts almost invariably have to fall back on damages in cases of large-scale pollution, an outcome that may equally result in halting the activity because of bankruptcy. There is, however, no guarantee that damages will be used to clean up pollution and end the nuisance. Take the case of Mr Tipping. Without an injunction, the noxious vapours would not have been stopped, as he had no access to the factory chimneys; if, on the other hand, damages had been awarded, he could simply have sold up and left with his money; he could not have been required to use them for clean-up purposes.

These are reasons why, in the Preamble of the latest EU Directive on environmental liability, the European Commission backs away from liability in tort. For many years the Commission has been discussing environmental liability, leaning to strict liability in an effort to "make the polluter pay". The recent Directive 2004/35/CE on environmental liability with regard to the prevention and remedying of environmental damage focuses on *prevention and remedy* and leaves the question of individual compensation to existing law. A duty is laid on anyone who operates or controls an economic activity, business or undertaking to take action to prevent environmental damage or to remedy it if it has occurred. The operator will bear the costs. Significantly, the Directive leaves the law of liability untouched.

We are now in a position to answer the questions posed at the start of this chapter. The lines drawn by the common law around the use and enjoyment of land are not drawn in the right place for our post-modern and post-industrial society. The way to deal with this is not, however, by extensions to the common law. The tort of nuisance is no substitute for detailed regulation of land use and pollution. A law of hazardous activity cannot be fashioned from the rule in *Rylands*. In the post-modern, post-industrialised society, in which an ever greater percentage of the population lives and works in big cities, regulation of the environment is essential. All that the common law can contribute is the limited regulation of relationships between neighbours.

FURTHER READING

Judges rely heavily on two seminal articles by Newark, "The Boundaries of Nuisance" (1949) 65 *Law Quarterly Review* 480 and "Non-Natural User and *Rylands v Fletcher*" (1961) 24 *Modern Law Review* 557. The student who wishes to understand these torts should follow their example. Brenner's spirited article, "Nuisance Law and the Industrial Revolution" (1973) 3 *Journal of Legal Studies* 403 gives a historical, contextual insight, as does the powerful response by McLaren, "Nuisance Law and the Industrial Revolution—Some Lessons from Social History" (1983) 3 *Oxford Journal of Legal Studies* 155. Ogus and Richardson, "Economics and the Environment: A Study of Private Nuisance" (1977) *Cambridge Law Journal* 284 still provides the best introduction to economic analysis of environmental torts. Steele, "Private Law and the Environment: Nuisance in Context" (1995) 15 *Legal Studies* 236 and Wilkinson, "*Cambridge Water Company v Eastern Counties Leather plc*: Diluting Liability for Continuing Escapes" (1994) 57 *Modern Law Review* 799 open up the modern issues. Their articles contain further references.

6

BUSINESS AND ECONOMIC INTERESTS

LAISSEZ-FAIRE AND FREEDOM OF CONTRACT

In the earlier chapters of this book, the evolution of tort law has been described largely in historical terms. A set of ancient, nominate torts exists, which typically protect selected interests. The cracks between the torts are papered over by negligence, at the same time a nominate tort and the general principle of civil liability. Interests in person and property are dominant. Tort law, in other words, protects what is tangible and physical. We have occasionally caught glimpses of other, less tangible interests. Pecuniary loss, such as loss of earnings or the expense of repairing vehicles, is recoverable in a road accident claim; in medical negligence litigation, we met the concept of "loss of a chance"; nuisance covers loss of amenity; and so on. We sensed, however, that once the common law is asked to step outside these limited categories, tort law is markedly less protective. Attempts to expand the nominate torts to protect new interests often failed, as with the use of nuisance to protect privacy (*Khorasandjian*, see above, p.15).

Some ancient property torts did protect the more tangible manifestations of emerging trade and industry: trespass to goods, for example, provided compensation for the destruction or seizure of stock-in-trade or tools, while the specialised writ of detinue provided for their return. By the sixteenth century, other specialised torts had extended the protection afforded to business interests. Injurious falsehood extended the protections of defamation to false statements causing financial losses, as where it is asserted that the claimant's firm has gone out of business or that his produce does not live up to the claims made for it in advertisement. The torts of conversion and slander of title protected title to goods, making it a tort to deal wrongfully in stolen goods or otherwise deny ownership and title. The Torts (Interference with Goods) Act 1977 modernised and codified some of these ancient torts. Coverage of economic interests was patchy and the emphasis on writs and forms of action left the law reliant on the old, common law notion of property as tangible, and slow to extend protection to intangible economic interests, such as loss of profits.

Cane provides a simple definition of economic interest as one "for which a finite sum of money can provide complete recompense" (Cane, 1996, p.5). Physical or property interests can be recompensed by damages but not completely. There may be a market, say, in human kidneys but loss of a kidney is not a purely economic loss. Economic interests are intangible and, in modern societies, wealth is more often intangible than tangible. We do not deal in gold bullion; we deal in stocks and shares. Our stake in land manifests itself in mortgages, leases and financial interests in property that we do not own. Our wealth lies in intellectual property: trade secrets, copyright, patents and franchises. Information—a form of intellectual property—is stored, accessed and exchanged on the internet. Goods are bought and sold on the internet using credit cards and contracts are concluded electronically. These are intangible economic interests, most of which can be fully recompensed by money but not all. Certain forms of intellectual property demand something more: money could not, for instance, wholly compensate for infringement of a trade name or misuse of cultural goods. Cane's definition is helpful but not entirely exhaustive.

Stock and machinery was one thing but when it came to intellectual property the courts were uncommonly slow to intervene. Today, someone who passes on information obtained in the course of an employment or other relationship of trust, whether to competitors or to the media, is in serious danger of being held liable for "breach of confidence". This new tort—if it is a tort and not a purely equitable remedy—originated in 1848 with an application to restrain unauthorised reproduction of engravings by Queen Victoria (*Prince Albert v Strange*, 1848). It was not until the 1970s, however, that a body of case law began to emerge to protect trade secrets (Vickery, 1982). Again, the tort of deceit was relevant to commercial dealings, supplementing the law of contract by providing damages for misrepresentation. The tort was, however, severely restricted by a nineteenth-century House of Lords decision, in which it was held that damages for loss caused by publication of misleading statements in a prospectus were available only on proof of fraud (*Derry v Peek*, 1889). Buyers and investors had to wait nearly a century for redress in cases of negligent misrepresentation (see now *Hedley Byrne*; s.2 of the Misrepresentation Act 1967).

The explanation—though not necessarily a justification—for these decisions has much to do with laissez-faire economic theory, which fostered a presumption that losses attributable to free trade and competition should not be recoverable. The case law crystallised in the late nineteenth century and behind the restrictive attitudes lies a fairly coherent economic ideology. The collective judicial mind was dominated—there were of course exceptions—by the vision of a market economy in which there would be an economic free-for-all. It would be the privilege and the obligation of everyone involved to protect themselves and their interests by entering into contracts. If this meant that the weakest—generally the worker and the consumer—went to the wall, this was healthy and in the interests of society at large. Commerce was properly the territory of contract, governed by the maxim of *caveat emptor* or "buyer beware". Until the intervention of *Donoghue*, contract generally trumped tort, leaving the consumer of defective goods without any practical remedy. Exemption clauses in standard form contracts were also barriers to tortious liability. Where contract would not provide a remedy, tort was often impotent as well—a point that emerges all too clearly from *Derry*.

COURTS, PARLIAMENT AND ECONOMIC TORTS

During the nineteenth century, however, a number of new economic torts were coming into being that could have taken tort law in a very different direction. A new tort, which came to be called *wrongful interference with contract*, was, for example, developed in *Lumley v Gye* (1853). L, the proprietor of Her Majesty's Theatre, had engaged Miss W as a singer. G persuaded her to abandon the engagement, enticing her away to sing at Drury Lane. Surprisingly, in the light of what has been said earlier, the court held actionable a deliberate and intentional act, which had the effect of causing damage to L by interfering with his contract. Here tort was invoked to buttress the "sanctity of contract" in a situation where, later writers argue, contract should have been left to distribute the risks. The case was, however, exceptional, the general situation being that neither contract nor tort was allowed in to regulate dubious trade practices.

Action against unfair competition was further handicapped by the rule that conduct does not become unlawful *merely because* it is aimed at harming another's economic interests (*Bradford v Pickles*, 1895; *Allen v Flood*, 1898). In a classic case that seriously restricted the development of the common law in this area, the House of Lords held that a group of dealers could band together to lower tea prices below what was profitable, with the aim of putting a competitor out of business; this was nothing more, they held, than an act designed to protect their own "legitimate interests" (*Mogul Steamship Co v McGregor, Gow, & Co*, 1892). From one angle, the case, which set in stone the principle that everyone has the right to conduct business to suit his own requirements even if the consequence is interference with other people's business, can be seen as having been decided in the interests of free trade. Today it would probably be viewed as encouraging the development of a monopoly, able to charge whatever price the trader pleases. The nineteenth-century judiciary seemed impervious to the fact that monopolies and cartels strike at the roots of free trade. As late as 1994, a judge was saying:

"There is no tort of taking a man's market or customers. Neither the market nor the customers are the plaintiff's to own. There is no tort of making use of another's goodwill as such. There is no tort of competition." (*Hodgkinson & Corby v Wards Mobility Services*, 1994, Jacob J.)

A significant factor in the uneven development was the growth of trade unions and judicial hostility to them. The development of the economic torts has been seriously one-sided: new torts evolved for the protection of employers against the workforce were not utilised to penalise business competitors. As Hepple, Howarth and Matthews put it:

"The economic torts largely developed in the sphere of industrial conflict, in which the fundamental problem has always been the incompatibility of collective industrial action with the individualist notions underpinning much of the nineteenth-century common law." (2002, p.851)

The tort of *conspiracy*, for example, can be traced to a handful of early "special actions on the case", designed simply to punish intentional interference with trade. It sprang into prominence at the end of the nineteenth century, in the context of collective industrial action, to penalise what judges called "a combination". At first the Lords took the line that motive alone was not enough to render lawful acts unlawful (*Allen v Flood*); very soon, however, they changed course (*Quinn v Leathem*, 1901). The use of unlawful means to carry out a lawful purpose was ruled unlawful and the law was complicated by the difficulty that "unlawful" had no fixed meaning. Criminal acts were unlawful but it was unclear whether the term covered breach of contract, and where tort was concerned, the terminology was quite simply circular: to declare actions tortious immediately rendered them unlawful, and vice versa. Tension arose between the courts and Parliament, as statute was used to immunise trade unions from liability for economic loss caused by industrial action: the Trade Disputes Act 1906, passed specifically to nullify a decision of the House of Lords, set a precedent. Courts fought back with ingenious extensions of old torts and even new torts to circumvent the statutory immunities. The consequence is a law so esoteric and hard to follow that the judges themselves cannot fully understand it. The boundaries of conspiracy are still uncertain. For liability to accrue there must be damage and the "predominant purpose" of conspirators must be to inflict that damage: but whether a purpose is predominant; whether it must also be unlawful; whether recourse to unlawful means is sufficient for liability; what means and what purposes are unlawful, are all contestable. The outlines of the tort change, like the amoeba, from case to case.

Over the past century, the ambit of the economic torts has in fact significantly broadened and several new torts have been spawned. In *Rookes v Barnard* (1964), trade union officials, for the purpose of enforcing a "closed shop" agreement that they had with management, put pressure on BOAC to dismiss R after he had resigned from the union. In breach of a "no strike" clause in their contracts, they threatened to strike. BOAC dismissed R, though not unlawfully because the correct period of notice was given. The situation did not fall within the tort of inducing breach of contract because no breach of contract took place. R therefore sued for conspiracy, the question being whether the union had used "unlawful means" to achieve its aims. The Court of Appeal answered this question in the negative and went on to rule out intimidation as a cause of action, as no threats of violence were involved. The House of Lords, accepting the first but not the second proposition, held that any threat or pressure to do something "not in itself lawful" amounts to intimidation. Combining elements of conspiracy with inducement of breach of contract, the House of Lords had created a new tort. The Labour Government then in power intervened immediately with the Trade Disputes Act 1965 to grant unions immunity from liability, though it did not reverse the decision in *Rookes* nor did it excise the tort of intimidation from the common law; this remained on the books to be developed into new heads of tortious liability. It casts a new light on a relationship in which the judiciary frequently describes itself as the junior partner, that the judges' view effectively prevailed.

Labour lawyers point to the contrast with the way in which these elusive economic torts operate in a non-union context. In *Lonrho v Shell Petroleum* (1982), Lonrho claimed £100 million in an action against Shell Petroleum in respect of revenue lost after Shell had closed down the refinery from which it supplied petroleum to Lonrho's pipeline. Shell's defence lay in an Order in Council imposing sanctions on Rhodesia, where the refinery was sited, after that colony had unlawfully made a unilateral declaration of independence. Lonrho, maintaining that Shell had acted behind the scenes in defiance of the order, supplying petroleum to Rhodesia by other means, alleged conspiracy and breach of statutory duty. The House of Lords held that no action lay as Shell's activities were designed "predominantly for their own purposes" and not "aimed at" Lonrho. The ingredients of conspiracy were by now "too well-established to be discarded". Yet 10 years later, in the course of a long-running battle over a takeover of Harrods, the London department store, by the Fayed brothers, the ground had to be retrodden (*Lonrho v Fayed*, 1992). This time Lonrho alleged the generic tort of "interference with business by unlawful means". The claim was unsuccessful but Lord Templeman somewhat wearily admitted that—without wishing to encourage further litigation from Lonrho—"the torts of conspiracy and unlawful interference may hereafter require further analysis and reconsideration by the courts".

TIDYING UP

Attitudes to trade and commercial activity have changed very markedly in the last half-century, as Lord Diplock, remarking on the fear of "combinations" that infused the common law, pointed out in *Lonrho v Shell*:

"[T]o suggest today that acts done by one street-corner grocer in concert with a second are more oppressive and dangerous to a competitor than the same acts done by a string of supermarkets under a single ownership or that a multinational conglomerate such as Lonrho or oil company such as Shell or BP does not exercise greater economic power than any combination of small businesses is to shut one's eyes to what has been happening in the business world since the turn of the century and, in particular, since the end of the 1939–45 war."

The Conservative victory of 1979 sent industrial relations into a new mode. The newly elected government quickly passed the Employment Act 1980, the first of several Acts designed severely to restrict trade union immunity in tort, a situation that still obtains. Meanwhile, competition is regulated by the European Union, which outlaws unfair competition and entrenches the notion of a "level playing field" for trade. Under the aegis of the EU, statute now regulates unfair consumer contracts. The potential for attacks on cartels and monopolies comes from concepts familiar in civilian legal systems, such as "abuse of a dominant position" and "abuse of rights" (Carty, 1988). In *Garden Cottage Foods v Milk Marketing Board* (1984), a small business dealing in the purchase and sale of bulk butter received notification from the Milk Marketing Board, a statutory agency responsible for around 75 per cent of butter production in the United Kingdom, that it would no longer be supplied. Article 82 (ex 86) of the EC Treaty forbids the abuse of a dominant position in the market and the article had already been held by the European Court of Justice to give rise to directly effective rights for individuals. The violation of EU law was classified by the House of Lords as a new form of breach of statutory duty for tort law purposes. Under EU influence too, the common law passing-off action, which protects trade names and trade marks, has taken on a new lease of life, making it tortious to describe a drink as "elder flower champagne" (*Bulmer v Bollinger*, 1974); Champagne is now a trade name.

This tidying-up process could be taken further. In *Lonrho v Fayed*, the Court of Appeal was broadly sympathetic to a new "genus tort" of "interference with the business of another by unlawful means" or, more simply, "wrongful interference with trade or business", though it hesitated to list the ingredients. There are English precedents. Something similar was proposed in *Mogul v McGregor* (1889) by Bowen L.J., who said

"Now intentionally to do that which is calculated in the ordinary course of events to damage, and which does in fact damage, another in that person's property or trade is actionable if done without just cause or excuse."

Note the relationship to the principle in *Wilkinson*, that an act wilfully done and calculated to cause physical harm, which does in fact cause physical harm, is actionable. This simple and flexible principle, which has in the United States been called "the prima facie tort doctrine" (Holmes, 1894), is quite as capable of development as Lord Atkin's famous neighbour principle of *Donoghue*. Yet the courts hesitate to apply it. Why?

Perhaps the courts do not wish to foster competition with negligence, the general principle of civil liability. Perhaps, however, they are simply unimaginative, especially in their use of comparative law (Markesinis and Deakin, 1992). Borrowing from continental legal terminology, we could argue that, to stand strictly on one's legal rights and exercise them for an improper or anti-social purpose is "an abuse of right". To put this differently, in some continental legal systems, rights are not absolute but limited: they can only be exercised in a way which accords with the public interest and to exceed these limits is an actionable abuse of right (Gutteridge, 1906). The abuse of rights principle covers cases like *Bradford*, where a landowner, unsuccessful in his negotiations to sell his land to the council for its water supply, deliberately drained the water off so that the council could not use it. It could also cover wrongful interference with trade or business. To introduce this principle would do a great deal to simplify and demystify the law. It would, however, greatly expand the range of tort law, enhancing judicial discretion in areas where it has not to date been used especially well.

NEGLIGENCE AND ECONOMIC LOSSES

Where pure economic losses are concerned, the negligence principle has not proved much more successful in simplifying the law than the nominate torts whose development we have just been criticising. Where economic loss is closely tied to physical damage, there is no special difficulty in recovering damages in negligence; both actual and potential loss of earnings can, for example, be recovered in a personal injuries action. The problem lies in the attitude of the common law or courts to "pure" economic loss, by which is meant simply loss unrelated to person or property. The courts looked on claims for economic losses with a suspicious eye. The "floodgates" argument is prevalent, according to which actions for economic loss open the door to "liability in an indeterminate amount for an indeterminate time to an indeterminate class" (*Ultramares v Touche*, Cardozo J.).

Before the days of mass torts, when products liability actions began to be brought against the multinational corporations, which today disseminate their goods globally; and before the nuclear disaster at Chernobyl raised the spectre of transcontinental damage to person and property; the courts knew where to draw the line and why. They believed that "only a limited amount of damage can ever ensue from a single act, while the number of economic interests a tortfeasor may destroy in a brief moment of carelessness is practically limitless". Lord Denning, speaking in a case involving the negligence of contractors, who had severed a cable supplying electricity to the claimant's works, remarked of a severed power line that it

"affects a multitude of persons; not as a rule by way of physical damage to them or their property, but by putting them to inconvenience, and sometimes to economic loss. The supply is usually restored in a few hours, so the economic loss is not very large. Such a hazard is regarded by most people as a thing they must put up with—without seeking compensation from anyone. Some there are who install a stand-by system. Others seek refuge by taking out an insurance policy against breakdown in the supply. But most people are content to take the risk on themselves. When the supply is cut off, they do not go running round to their solicitor. They do not try to find out whether it was anyone's fault. They just put up with it. They try to make up the economic loss by doing more work next day. This is a healthy attitude which the law should encourage." (*Spartan Steel and Alloys Ltd v Martin*, 1973)

Lord Denning was expressing in everyday language the idea that the reallocation of economic losses, though no doubt lucrative, is not a profitable activity for courts. It creates risks that cannot easily be insured against or, if they can, the policies cannot be afforded. The losses will be smaller and perhaps less damaging if they are shared between victims. First-party loss insurance may here be more realistic and fairer than third-party liability insurance: the owners of a deep-freeze might, for example, insure against an interruption of current, and "business interruption" policies also exist which cater for this type of eventuality. Like Lord Denning, the courts have tended to assume that it is not only fairer but also economically more efficient to spread the load.

But why should this be? It is not the case with personal injuries actions. The rise of the mass tort or class action also creates the prospect of "liability in an indeterminate amount for an indeterminate time to an indeterminate class". It is not felt, however, that it would be more economically efficient to let the losses lie where they fall; to the contrary, the response of the courts has rather been to facilitate litigation (*Fairchild v Glenhaven Funeral Services*, see above, p.71). It is hard to explain or justify the difference, which lends cogency to the argument that all forms of loss should receive identical treatment: in other words that the standard negligence test of foreseeability should apply. Although the courts have been inching the law in this direction, this point has never yet been reached.

TORT VERSUS CONTRACT

Moreover, not every action for economic loss does have the ripple effect referred to by Lord Denning. In Ch.2, we looked at *Hedley Byrne*, where a firm of advertisers sued bankers in respect of a negligently worded reference. There was no contract; the bankers voluntarily undertook to give the reference, although, fortunately for them, they added a proviso that they undertook no responsibility for its accuracy, which proved enough to preclude liability. But the House of Lords went on to hold that a limited duty of care existed. They were not on the face of things opening a floodgate. The reference was intended only for one person and, in any event, allowing liability to be restricted had provided an escape route. "It would be one thing", said Lord Reid, "to say that the speaker owes a duty to a limited class but it would be going very far to say that he owes a duty to every ultimate 'consumer' who acts on these words to his detriment." This suggests that, at the date of the decision, the House of Lords did not grasp the full implications of *Hedley Byrne*. It was not self-evident that liability could extend beyond the two parties involved in the transaction. It was not clear how far the way would be opened to claims for economic loss. It was far from obvious too that the boundary lines between contract and tort would be threatened and might have to be redrawn.

The reason why *Hedley Byrne* posed a far greater threat to contract than *Donoghue* lies in the fact that it was a case of "pure" economic loss. There was no property loss or physical injury; the damage consisted of loss suffered when clients, whose accounts

Hedley Byrne had underwritten on the strength of a misleading reference, were unable to pay. The applicable tort rule was that in *Derry* (above): the loss was, in short, only recoverable on proof of fraud or deceit. The House of Lords took tort law out of line with contract, allowing tort to trump contract: despite the clear contractual rules about consideration, they had allowed the claimants to sue on a gratuitous undertaking, for which no consideration had been given. It is interesting to compare the two leading judgments of Lords Reid and Devlin. The first uses the imagery of tort law, redefining the classic "neighbour" test in terms of a "special relationship" characterised by the "reliance" of one party on the other. The reasoning of the second is much closer to contract; crudely to summarise, Lord Devlin envisages liability in cases where there is almost, but not quite, a contract. This created an inducement for someone discontented with his bargain to bypass the rules of contract by framing his action in tort. In the key case of *Esso Petroleum v Mardon* (1976), the Court of Appeal opened the door to "picking and choosing". M, the prospective tenant of a petrol station, had asked Esso, the owner and supplier, what his profits were likely to be. Negligently, Esso gave a wholly inaccurate picture. Relying on their expertise, M leased the station, subsequently losing all his savings when petrol purchases failed to reach the estimated figure. Contract afforded no remedy, as the misrepresentation had not been incorporated as a term of the contract; instead, the Court of Appeal allowed recovery in a tort action for negligent advice. The door had been kicked wide open and the courts would need to find solutions for the problems of economic loss in tort.

This case tells us that the standard of conduct expected from the defendant is not necessarily the same in contract and tort. Tort remedies are open to third parties and the standard of care is usually that of the reasonable man; in contract, it is the standard bargained for. This particular contract might, for example, have required Shell to "warrant" the accuracy of the information given to Mr Mardon—though given the unequal standing of the parties, this is unlikely. More probably, it was silent on the point. Contractual warranties may be stricter, in that goods offered for sale must be fit for the purpose for which they are intended and contractual actions lie not only for physical injury but for economic losses; on the other hand, they are open only to the purchaser in an action against the vendor. Consumer contracts are subject to standards settled by a series of Sale of Goods Acts that the goods will be fit for the purpose for which they have been purchased. Tort law imposes a different duty that they will not be "defective", which has been picked up by the legislator. What is important here is that the two duties are not identical.

This is not the place for a detailed study of the differences between tort and contract, but a few central differences have to be borne in mind. For example, it is important that the basis on which damages are calculated differs in tort and contract. In Ch.3, we saw that the test of liability for damage in tort law is foreseeability, according to the standard of the reasonable man. In contract, damages are supposed to mirror the expectations of the parties; in other words, to give the plaintiff no more and no less than what he bargained for (Adams and Brownsword, 2004, pp.154–167). Consequential losses—for example, the loss of profits resulting from a late delivery—are not recoverable unless the court considers that they were, in the classic phrase, "in the contemplation of the parties" when the contract was made (*Hadley v Baxendale*, 1854). The first test is objective, the second subjective, and they do not always bring the same results. The difference is often expressed by saying that in contract the plaintiff can claim *expectation damages*, including the loss of his bargain, while in tort the defendant has to restore the pre-existing position (Adams and Brownsword, 2004, pp.155–157). There may in practice be little difference but, in cases of economic loss, whether the action is framed in tort or contract may sometimes affect the outcome.

Winfield (1931b) described the obligations of tort law as "imposed by the law", meaning that they are general in their application. Central to contract is the concept of a *bargain*. Contractual obligations are assumed *voluntarily* or at least based on a situation where the parties' conduct allows consent to be implied (Adams and Brownsword, 2004, pp.14–17). While consent or presumed consent remains central to contract, in tort law it has largely lost its place (Atiyah, 1978). Contracts in English law must be supported by "consideration"; a mere promise is not enough for contract, there must be an exchange of economic assets (Adams and Brownsword, 2004, pp.74–87). The absence of consideration in *Hedley Byrne* lay behind Lord Devlin's idea of a contract that is not quite a contract. Lord Reid's use of "reliance" as a partial surrogate allowed the need for consideration to be circumvented. As with *Donoghue*, where the indirect impact of the case extended far beyond the parties, forming the basis of the modern law of products liability, so too the impact of *Hedley Byrne* has been wide-ranging.

According to the doctrine of "privity of contract", only the parties to a contract can sue on it; third parties cannot normally take the benefit of contracts to which they are not party (Adams and Brownsword, 2004, pp.87–93). Tort law helps to undermine this key limitation of contract. In *Ross v Caunters* (1979), disappointed beneficiaries claimed the value of their potential legacies when solicitors drew a will so negligently that it was invalid. Many years later, considering a similar situation, Lord Goff allowed "the impulse to do practical justice" to override conceptual difficulties of which he was very conscious (*White v Jones*, 1995). The problem lies in the triangular nature of the relationships. The testator could have sued the solicitor for breach of contract but (besides being dead) he has suffered no tangible loss. The beneficiaries, who have lost their legacies, are not in a contractual relationship with the solicitor. Imposing a duty of care allows the beneficiaries to obtain via tort the benefit of a contract to which they were not parties. Compare this with the rather similar situation of *Donoghue*, which involved a contractual chain. The vendor is liable to the purchaser, who has suffered no loss to speak of, and the manufacturer is liable in contract to the vendor. There may be a breach of a contractual warranty. The real damage was, however, suffered by a third party, who stood outside the contractual chain. By imposing a duty of care on the manufacturer, the difficulty of privity was circumvented.

In *Smith v Bush, Harris v Wyre Forest District Council* (1989), the issue was negligent valuations by two surveyors, the first acting for a building society, the second for a local authority. The reports were sent on to the purchasers (in the second case together with a disclaimer of liability), who purchased without a further survey. Structural defects missed by the surveyors later involved them in considerable expense. The House of Lords thought that a surveyor valuing a "small house" or "modest home" for a building society or local authority ought to foresee that the purchaser is likely to act on his report; consequently, the relationship is sufficiently proximate for a duty of care to exist. Lord Templeman cited a government Green Paper, which required those practising conveyancing to insure. He also suggested that in these circumstances it would be hard for professional conveyancers to contract out of liability. The Unfair Contract Terms Act 1977 now provides that a disclaimer of liability must "satisfy the requirement of reasonableness" and Lord Templeman thought it "not fair and reasonable for building societies and valuers to agree together to impose on purchasers the risk of loss arising as a result of incompetence or carelessness on the part of valuers". Clearly these cases have very wide implications for all professionals, such as lawyers, financial advisers or accountants, who deal in advice that may cause financial losses and equally wide implications for their insurers. Since they were decided, the liability of professionals has expanded at a dizzying speed until "solicitors and other professionals find themselves liable not only to their own clients in ways they had not previously envisaged, but increasingly to non-clients" (Walford, 2002). The process has—for the time being—culminated in *Arthur S. Hall v Simons* (1999), where the well-established immunity in negligence of advocates was summarily demolished, exposing solicitor advocates to potentially wide liability.

Many of the economic loss cases involve investors, who find they have made a bad bargain. This was essentially the situation in *Henderson v Merrett Syndicates* (1994). Lloyd's "names" are investors in the reinsurance market, who share the profits in good times and pay out in bad. After suffering substantial losses, the "names" sued the managing agents of the Lloyd's syndicates for negligence in the management of their affairs. The agents argued that their liability should be confined to contract but the House of Lords, applying *Hedley Byrne,* ruled that a duty of care in tort existed. The principles established in such cases can go much further, endangering regulators. In *The Nicholas H* (1996), a ship sank after a private classification society allowed it to go to sea in an unseaworthy condition and the owners of the cargo sought compensation. *Yuen Kun-yeu*, a case that we have met already in the context of incrementalism (see above, p.59), concerned a statutory official, who exercised supervisory powers over deposit-taking companies in Hong Kong. Neither action was successful; in economic loss cases, the courts seem unwilling to transfer losses to peripheral parties (McLean, 1998). The *Three Rivers* case (2000) is similar. It concerns the obligations of the Bank of England, acting under statutory powers, to supervise the activities of a private bank, the BCCI, which went bankrupt, causing substantial economic losses to clients, investors and employees. The difference here lies in the attempt to invoke the specialised tort of misfeasance in public office against the autonomous Bank of England (Andenas and Fairgrieve, 2002; see below, p.142).

The parties to these cases are merchants and industrialists, advised by lawyers, well-versed in the law, experienced in bargaining and accustomed to regulating their affairs by contract. One reason why the courts ruled out tortious liability in the complex *Keyser Ullmann* litigation, involving fraud perpetrated

against a bank, on the ground that failure to disclose facts in pre-
contractual negotiations is not actionable in contract, may be that
the parties were banks, insurers and insurance brokers. Many of
the cases concern shipping, a highly specialised branch of law governed by the Hague Rules, an international convention, where the
courts hesitate to intervene. In *The Aliakmon* (1986), where the
courts were asked to lay down a general rule for the recovery of
economic loss in a very complex shipping case involving economic
damage done to goods before the legal property had passed, Lord
Brandon had this to say:

"[It was] submitted that any rational system of law ought to provide a remedy for persons who suffered the kind of loss which the
buyers suffered in the present case, with the clear implication
that, if your Lordships' House were to hold that the remedy . . .
was not available, it would be lending its authority to an irrational feature of English law. I do not agree with this submission
for, as I shall endeavour to show, English law does, in all normal
cases, provide a fair and adequate remedy for loss of or damage
to goods the subject of a [standard shipping] contract, and the
buyers in this case could easily, if properly advised at the time
when they agreed to the variation of the original . . . contract,
have secured to themselves the benefit of such a remedy."

While there must be much sympathy with this viewpoint, it is
hardly likely to stem the flow of litigation. Balked in their action
against the ship-owners, buyers are likely to spell out of Lord
Brandon's words a cause of action against their legal advisers.

In the context of moves towards a law of obligations, blurring
of the contract/tort boundary may seem acceptable. By and large,
however, the commentators do not find it so. Atiyah (1978) advocates a radical restructuring around the classic concepts of
"reliance" and "voluntary undertaking" common, in his view, to
both contract and tort. Recovery of economic loss would then be
possible only where the claimant had *relied* on the defendant. This
mode of reasoning finds a place in *Henderson*, which based liability on "assumption of responsibility" by the agents. Once tort law
moves to assess these concepts *objectively*, however, they add
little to the "fair, just and reasonable" test of *Caparo* (see above,
p.59). In this case, C had purchased shares on the basis of audited
accounts that showed a company to be profitable when it was in
fact making losses. Reining back, the House of Lords ruled that
there was insufficient proximity between the parties for liability.

But why are auditors not responsible for the accuracy of their accounts when purchasers are able to rely on surveyors? Are the distinctions in these cases really tenable? Stapleton (1994) asks for a new set of bright lines to guide those who have to struggle with economic loss cases. But where should they be drawn?

Other authors frame their answers more directly in terms of the contract/tort boundary. McGrath (1985) suggested restricting liability narrowly to cases where (as in *Hedley Byrne*) there has been negligent performance of a voluntarily assumed undertaking— the "contract that is not quite a contract" idea. In this way liability could normally be narrowed to a small class of claimants who would be entirely foreseeable. This tallies with Atiyah's more ambitious proposition for a new law of obligations, which would fuse the traditional rules of tort and contract where necessary. Fleming (1992) approaches the matter from the contract angle, arguing that the integrity of contract must be maintained. His solution is to restrict liability in tort wherever significant contract rules concerning damages, privity or warranties would be undercut; in other words, the bright line would be drawn to rule out "picking and choosing". This is sound advice but is not the direction in which the courts have consistently travelled. Bishop (1982), in an economic analysis, is more robust, recommending that the judges select a theory of loss allocation and stick to it!

All that we can conclude is that tort law as yet provides only limited protection for economic interests and that the circumstances in which it does this remain unsystematic and occasionally ill-considered. The growth of the economic torts has been marred by their one-sided development and historic hostility to industrial action. On another level, the law is flawed by the absence of an underlying general principle of liability, such as is found in continental systems. Negligence liability has been allowed to drift "incrementally" from case to case, with consequential damage to the contract/tort boundary. Sometimes tort, sometimes contract, seems to be in the ascendant and a final solution seems out of the reach of the courts. Essentially, Bishop is right in demanding a more theoretical approach.

FURTHER READING

The economic torts are dealt with very fully and with enviable clarity in Ch.15 of Hepple, Howarth and Matthews' *Tort Cases and Materials* (5th ed., London, Butterworths, 2000), where you will find ample suggestions for further reading. Atiyah's theory, mentioned in the text, is set out in "Contracts, Promises and the Law of Obligations" (1978) 94 *Law Quarterly Review* 193. Useful introductions to the contract/tort problem, though a little dated, are by Holyoak, "Tort and Contract after *Junior Books*" (1983) 99 *Law Quarterly Review* 591 and Jaffey, "Contract in Tort's Clothing" (1984) *Legal Studies* 77. Bishop's economic theory is contained in "Economic Loss in Tort" (1982) 2 *Oxford Journal of Legal Studies* 1. Feldthusen, "The Recovery of Pure Economic Loss in Canada: Proximity, Justice, Rationality and Chaos" (1996) 24 *Manitoba Law Journal* 1 lends a comparative dimension, as do Markesinis and Deakin, "The Random Element of their Lordships' Infallible Judgement: An Economic and Comparative Analysis of the Tort of Negligence from *Anns* to *Murphy*" (1992) 55 *Modern Law Review* 561. Whittaker, "Privity of Contract and the Tort of Negligence: Future Directions" (1996) 16 *Oxford Journal of Legal Studies* 191 focuses on privity. Cane's full-length study, *Tort Law and Economic Interests* (2nd ed., Oxford, Clarendon, 1996) is comprehensive and clear.

7

RIGHTS TALK

To the modern reader, brought up in an era of "rights talk", it will not seem surprising if tort law protects human rights. The real surprise lies in finding that it does not—or at least, not directly. Some fundamental rights or civil liberties are in fact strongly protected by the common law: right to life, liberty and freedom from torture are, for example, human rights covered by the trespass torts, which also cover wrongful arrest, detention and false imprisonment (see Ch.8). From time to time, we have come across other cases involving civil liberties or human rights. In *DPP v Jones* (1999), we saw for instance that the common law recognised freedom of association and assembly but at the same time gave relatively weak protection to this important civil liberty. The suggestion was made that the law in this area might need rebalancing and could receive reinforcement from the right of association protected by Art.11 of the European Convention on Human Rights (ECHR).

Person and property are tangible interests, strongly protected by the common law. Liberty and freedom of association are intangible interests, which cannot be touched or, unlike economic interests, quantified. Just as the common law protects economic interests only sporadically, it protects other intangible interests more sporadically still. The case of *Ashby v White* (1703) is justly celebrated because the right to vote was unexpectedly recognised as a protected interest. It is nonetheless significant that the principle was contained in a dissenting judgment and that the decision was contestable at the time. This chapter shows how the common law defines human dignity almost solely in terms of reputation; even extensions into privacy are hotly debated—a controversy we have already met in Ch.1. Protected by the Court of Appeal in *Khorasandjian v Bush* (1993) through an extension to the law of nuisance, the right to privacy was disavowed by the House of Lords for technical reasons in *Hunter v Canary Wharf* (1997). We shall pick this argument up later in the chapter.

Today we would probably view privacy as one of a family of interests rooted in the concepts of human dignity and autonomy, fashionable values that are coming to the forefront of human rights discourse and are singled out by many human rights texts as the most fundamental of human rights (see Feldman, 1999). Human dignity has many aspects other than privacy. Highly rated, for example, in our multicultural societies is the right not to be discriminated against, weakly protected by the common law and weakly protected too by ECHR Art.14, which treats the right as parasitic: in other words, discrimination is forbidden only where another Convention-protected right is violated. *Statutory torts of discrimination in the context of employment have had to be created by the British Parliament and are contained in the Race Relations Act 1976 and Sex Discrimination Act 1975.*

Of the many rights documents to which the United Kingdom subscribes, none are directly enforceable in our courts nor do they create new torts. The ECHR allows the "victim" of a violation of the Convention to complain to the European Court of Human Rights but this arrangement, which leaves remedy to the national authorities and national legal system, does contain two "fallback" provisions that bear indirectly on damages in national courts

- ECHR Art.13 provides that an "effective remedy" must be available in cases of violation of the Convention;

- ECHR Art.41 allows the European Court of Human Rights to make an order affording "just satisfaction" to an injured party where it feels that the national system affords only a partial remedy (Mowbray, 2001).

The Human Rights Act, which "brought rights home" in 1998 and came into force two years later, annexes selected articles of the ECHR to the Act, giving them binding force. Section 8 of the Human Rights Act leaves the question of damages open, providing that the court may grant "such relief or remedy as it considers appropriate", a formula that can include damages. Damages are, however, only available where the court is satisfied that "the award is necessary to afford just satisfaction to the person in whose favour it is made". As Fairgrieve (2002, p.54) observes, it is "more accurate to describe this as a new *power* to award damages for unlawfulness. It is difficult to describe this new action as a public law tort if there is no *right* to monetary compensation." In short, the ambiguous formulation stops short of creating a human rights tort. We saw this point indirectly illustrated in the *Marcic* case, discussed in Ch.5. Mr Marcic, whose loss when sewage flooded his garden is best characterised as *property* damage, rested his case in part on ECHR Art.8(1), which combines tangible and intangible interests, providing that everyone has the right to "respect for his private and family life, his home and his correspondence". We saw that the Court of Appeal rejected the human rights argument, which could have been an oblique step towards a generic human rights tort, a development discussed in the last section of this chapter.

FREEZING FREE SPEECH

In modern Britain, freedom of speech and political opinion, together with press and media freedom, are highly valued as civil liberties of fundamental importance to democracy. ECHR Art.10 protects freedom of expression and opinion and also the "right to receive and impart information and ideas" but the rights are subject to a proviso, permitting them to be subjected to such restrictions as are "prescribed by law and necessary in a democratic society". Press freedom also receives specific mention in s.12 of the Human Rights Act, which requires a court in considering whether to grant a "prior restraint" injunction prohibiting publication to "have particular regard to the importance of the Convention right to freedom of expression". Section 13 of the Human Rights Act also makes special mention of conscience, opinion and religion, allowing religious bodies sometimes to discriminate positively in favour of their members. Article 10 can, as we are about to see, come into conflict with the common law tort of defamation. It can also come into conflict with other rights, notably the Art.8 right to privacy. These potential clashes involve the judges in difficult balancing acts.

It has been asserted that ECHR Art.10 is merely "an articulation of some of the principles underlying the common law" and that "freedom of speech has existed in this country perhaps as long as, if not longer than, it has existed in any other country in the world" (Loveland, 1994, p.221). If this is so, the United States Bill of Rights reinstated a common law value that had become heavily diluted in its country of origin. The common law tort of libel, which protected reputation, was never oriented towards free speech; its inglorious past is replete with authoritarian connotations. The Statute of Westminster 1275 actually created a special offence to protect the reputation of those who held high office from "false news or tales", to prevent "discord between the king and his people or the great men of the realm". We would call this a public order offence, the gravity of which lay in undercutting the authority of officials. For Blackstone (1787, p.150), the gist of the offence of criminal libel was its potential for breach of the peace "by stirring up the objects . . . to revenge, and perhaps to bloodshed"—again, essentially a public order offence.

Criminal libel is one of a stable of common law criminal offences, including blasphemy, obscenity and sedition. These, though seldom used, remain on the statute book. All are offences against the state, their gravity stemming from their tendency to undercut the authority of the state and public officials. That the various branches of seditious libel were developed and used oppressively by the hated prerogative Court of the Star Chamber in the sixteenth and seventeenth centuries was no coincidence. This was a period of great constitutional and political change. It was also the time that pamphlets and magazines were starting to be more widely circulated, making political writing more important. Throughout the eighteenth century, prosecutions for criminal libel were used to repress arguments for political and religious reform. Tom Paine's famous political tract, *The Rights of Man*, was prosecuted as a criminal libel, while *The Age of Reason* was the subject of a prosecution for blasphemy against the publisher. The wide use of the offences in this period forms part of a battle for freedom of speech and political opinion in which the enemy was the state in all its authoritarian manifestations.

This battle for free speech is strongly reflected in the First Amendment of the United States Constitution, enacted while the oppressive activity of the Star Chamber was very much alive in the memory of the American colonists. The First Amendment famously reads:

"Congress shall make no law respecting an establishment of religion, or prohibiting the free exercise thereof; or abridging the freedom of speech, or of the press; or the right of the people peaceably to assemble, and to petition the Government for a redress of grievances."

This transforms free speech into a constitutional right, explaining and justifying the more protective attitude of the American judiciary and the fiercer attitude to infringements of free speech typical of the American case law (Barendt, 1993). Note how this right diverges from ECHR Art.10, with its general proviso in para.2, and specific protection in para.1 for the licensing of "broadcasting television or cinema enterprises". Thus American law finds it difficult to prohibit "hate speech", or abuse directed at racial groups or political minorities (Abel, 1994). Although the tort of defamation does not cover hate speech, as its reach does not extend to groups or classes of unidentifiable individuals, it could, in countries governed by the ECHR, be easily outlawed under the proviso. (A specific offence of inciting racial hatred has indeed been introduced in the criminal law of the United Kingdom.)

Well before the Human Rights Act came into force, courts in the United Kingdom were increasingly feeling the influence of ECHR Art.10. A climate of opinion had evolved in which press freedom was highly valued as a democratic right. The trivial nature of many modern defamation cases also tended to darken its image "in the estimation of right thinking members of society". *Derbyshire County Council v Times Newspapers* (1993) marks a significant move in the direction of freeing up political comment. The council sought to sue *The Times*, which had alleged impropriety in the council's handling of its investments, for defamation. The House of Lords took the view that there was "no pressing social need" for a public authority to possess the right to sue in defamation; not only could the "reputation" of such a body be adequately defended by individual councillors but it was also "open to the controlling body to defend itself by public utterances and in debate in the council chamber". This judgment is premised on the need for free discussion of matters of general public interest and political importance and moves the common law far from the repressive ideology of criminal libel.

Thus far we have been talking of libel as a *criminal* offence but it is also one branch of the ancient *tort* of defamation, the other being slander. Libel was originally written, slander spoken. Today this has become a purely historical anomaly and one that the Faulks Committee, set up in 1975 to consider the need for simplification and change in the law of defamation, thought should be ended by amalgamating the two torts. The Committee suggested a new statutory tort of defamation, defined as "the publication to a third person of matter which in all the circumstances would be likely to affect a person adversely in the estimation of reasonable people generally" (Cmnd.5909, para.64). This would replace the traditional definition of a defamatory statement as one likely to cause a person to be "shunned or avoided"; exposed to "hatred, ridicule or contempt"; or, in the most traditional formulation, "discredited or lowered in the estimation of right thinking members of society generally". By now the reader will not be surprised to learn that this sensible recommendation has never been implemented.

Defences available to actions for defamation reflect both the battle for political freedom and the changing standards of public life. Thus statements made in the course of legal and parliamentary proceedings are absolutely privileged and cannot form the basis of a defamation action, both defences being well established by the seventeenth century. In 1689, the Bill of Rights put parliamentary privilege beyond doubt by providing in Art.9 that "freedom of speech, and debates or proceedings in Parliament ought not to be impeached or questioned in any court or place out of Parliament". This article still possesses a powerful, constitutional resonance, comparable to that of the First Amendment but with a rather different slant. Neither the individual MP nor the press is privileged; the privilege belongs to Parliament in its capacity of "the grand inquest of the nation" and while absolute parliamentary privilege can be abused—as Enoch Powell MP once observed, "That is what it is there for!"—it is for Parliament to punish abuse. In 1840, the Parliamentary Papers Act privileged full and accurate reports of parliamentary proceedings, an immunity maintained with a similar immunity for judicial proceedings by ss.13 and 14 of the Defamation Act 1996. This Act recognises our international obligations by extending privilege specifically to proceedings in the European Court of Justice and the European Court of Human Rights.

Two further defences protect political opinion at common law. The first is the defence of "fair comment", which covers all opinions honestly held provided they are based on true facts. A second common law defence of "qualified privilege" applies to a further range of situations where free speech is considered to be of public interest. These situations are of two types: some are based on purely private relationships, such as that which exists between the giver and recipient of a reference, where confidence is considered to be essential. Others are situations of public interest and range from abridged reports of judicial and parliamentary proceedings (extended by Sch.1 to the Defamation Act 1996 to the European Parliament and Member State legislatures) to complaints about and criticism of the conduct of public authorities, where the public interest requires that "publication to the world at large" should be privileged. The defence covers any situation where "the person to whom a statement is made has a special interest in learning the honestly held views of another person, even if those views are defamatory of someone else and cannot be proved to be true. Where the interest is of sufficient importance to outweigh the need to protect reputation, the occasion is regarded as privileged." (*Reynolds v Times Newspapers*, 2001)

Like fair comment, the defence can, however, be defeated if the claimant can prove malice. "Malice" in this context is more than a technicality; it covers both spite and reckless or wilful indifference to the falsity of a statement. In *Reynolds* a much wider privilege was demanded. On the resignation of Mr Reynolds as Prime Minister of Ireland, *The Times* published an article about his conduct in the post of Attorney-General, containing the innuendo that he had deliberately and dishonestly misled both the Irish Dáil and his Cabinet colleagues. The paper successfully persuaded the Court of Appeal to import the very famous American case of *New York Times v Sullivan* (1964). This creates the loose and unstructured defence of "generic qualified privilege", which extends to *all* "political material", where its "nature, status, source and the circumstances of publication" are "such as to merit a public interest defence". By a narrow majority, the House of Lords decided to restore the traditional test of common law qualified privilege, believing that its balance of duty versus interest provided adequate protection for both parties. In effect, the occasion of publication was one of qualified privilege but the defence could be defeated by proof of malice. Under the influence of ECHR Art.10, the judiciary can here be seen as "inching towards free speech" (Loveland 2000, p.357).

Advocates of press freedom argue that the rules expose the media to too great a threat of liability and act as a serious disincentive to investigation of the integrity of elected politicians. In fact, the claimant is probably the loser, as malice is notoriously difficult to prove. Moreover, the media do not always use their freedom well and jury trials suggest some public sympathy for the robust view of Lord Goodman, a practitioner with wide experience on both sides of the defamation fence:

"A great newspaper—if it believes that some villainy ought to be exposed—should expose it without hesitation and without regard to the law of libel. If the editor, his reporters and his advisers are men of judgment and sense, they are unlikely to go wrong; but if they do go wrong the principle of publish and be damned is a valiant and sensible one for the newspaper and it should bear the responsibility. Publish—and let someone else be damned—is a discreditable principle for a free press."

The freezing effects of defamation extend beyond the media and far beyond the author of a defamatory statement. It is not surprising to find the term "publication" covering editors of newspapers, publishers of books and producers of plays; it is more surprising to find that it extends to mere distributors, such as librarians, booksellers, distributors of films and owners of television networks. This may in practice put great pressure on authors, as standard terms in contracts of employment or for services require them to indemnify the publisher against inclusion of defamatory matter but also to allow the employer or distributor to take over the proceedings. The result may be that an action the author would prefer to defend is settled. The more distant figures can also be caught by the harsh rule of "innocent defamation" established in *Hulton v Jones* (1910). This term catches seemingly innocuous and straightforward statements, which may, given special knowledge, contain a hidden defamatory meaning or "innuendo". The caption to a photograph wrongly describing the subjects as married may, if they are not in fact married, be actionable by the true wife; a report that X has been convicted may, though strictly accurate, be actionable by a second, innocent Mr X; and so on.

Until the Defamation Act 1952 introduced the defence of apology, the publisher of an innocent defamation had no defence. Disseminators had the defence of "innocent dissemination", provided they could show they did not know that the offending material contained a libel or that the publication was "of a character to do so". This defence was cleverly exploited by Sir James Goldsmith in his private war against the satirical magazine *Private Eye*, when he took action against major retail outlets, arguing that, given the history of libel actions against *Private Eye*, bookstores ought to be on their guard (*Goldsmith v Sperrings Ltd*, 1977). Section 4 of the 1952 Act provided that, in cases of unintentional defamation, the publisher could make "an offer of amends" or apology where he did not know of any circumstances which might make the words defamatory of the claimant; unfortunately, the procedures proved too complicated to be easily used. The Defamation Act 1996 seeks to simplify the procedure, making it easier for the press to publish a correction with apology. It also puts in place for a publisher the double defence that he has taken "reasonable care" and proof that he "did not know, and had no reason to believe" that what he did had caused or contributed to the publication of a defamatory statement. The new defence was recently invoked in a case that brings defamation law into the world of 21st-century technology (*Godfrey v Demon Internet Ltd*, 1999). An internet service provider had transmitted an obscene message for posting in the claimant's name to DIL, a Usenet newsgroup. G had faxed, asking for the message to be removed as a forgery but this was not done. Once more distinguishing United States law, the judge ruled that, from the date of the fax, DIL could no longer fulfil the second condition that it "did not know and had no reason to believe" that it was participating in dissemination of defamatory matter. Internet defamation actions could provide much new work for lawyers!

COMPLEXITY AND COST

The real problems of defamation are complexity and cost. Costs soar because, although the Defamation Act 1996 now provides a summary procedure, defamation actions are usually tried by a judge and jury. Jury trial, once a protection against repressive state action, now affords a stage for soap operas in which politicians and television personalities voluntarily display in public the intimate details of their private lives; whatever the outcome, reputations are more likely to be lost than won. Much unnecessary litigation turns on the division of functions between judge and jury: whether a statement *is in fact defamatory* is the issue before the jury; whether it is *capable of bearing a defamatory meaning* is a matter for the judge. Judges remain wary of depriving the defendant of the right to jury trial by usurping the jury function and, if appellate courts feel that this has happened, a retrial may be granted, prolonging the litigation. Defamation has become an arcane and highly specialist area of tort law, where subtleties of pleading turn it into "the last refuge of complexity and technicality in the law". When a statement is not on its face defamatory, an "innuendo" must be pleaded, requiring the claimant to show that the words can be understood in a particular sense that he alleges to be defamatory. In practice, cases of innuendo often turn on technicalities of pleading, providing further opportunities for appeal.

The same is true of the defences of justification and fair comment, in both of which truth is an issue. Justification used to require the defendant to prove the truth of each and every one of the allegations made—an impossibly heavy burden now lightened by s.5 of the Defamation Act 1952, which allows the defendant to justify the main tenor or "sting" of the allegations made. This allows much room for manoeuvre by the skilled practitioner, who may deliberately omit to plead a true allegation in the hope of depriving the defendant of its defence. The defendant may respond by admitting that the article contains some small inaccuracies but justifying the "sting" of the remarks. In *Khashoggi v IPC Magazines* (1986), K was accused of sexual promiscuity, in an article listing a number of her lovers. The publisher pleaded justification, to which K responded that the list was inexact. The unpleasing battle of wits was of great importance, as it deprived K of her primary object: a "prior restraint" injunction, restraining publication pending trial.

The defence of fair comment can give rise to highly technical arguments over what is fact and what opinion. The sorry saga of *Telnikoff v Matusevitch* (1991) involved a dispute between two private individuals over a letter M had written to the *Daily Telegraph*, attacking an article by T as racist. T was awarded £65,000 damages in a jury trial, later set aside because he had not been represented. At the end of a new, two-day trial, the judge withdrew the case from the jury on technical grounds, ruling that any reasonable jury, properly directed, would be bound to uphold the defence of fair comment, since there was no evidence of express malice. This short cut proved costly! It took the House of Lords four days to decide whether the jury, in considering the defence of fair comment, ought to have looked only at M's letter or to have read it in conjunction with the original article. After 14 pages of judgement, the case was returned to a new jury for a partial retrial, with an order made for division of the costs. Bearing in mind that no legal aid is available in defamation cases, it is questionable whether the parties would have had sufficient funds to go on. That legal aid is not available can undoubtedly deter someone with a good case from suing, as in *Joyce v Sengupta* (1992), where J, Princess Anne's personal maid, who lost her job when *Today* published an article hinting that she had stolen intimate letters and leaked them to the press, was unable to sue for defamation because legal aid was not available. Instead she sued for the similar wrong of publishing an injurious falsehood, one of the economic torts briefly mentioned in Ch.6.

The chief effect of juries in modern defamation trials has been to escalate the scale of damages, decided by the jury and not the judge. Juries are notoriously generous with the funds of the press and the imprecise way in which damages are calculated allows them to make their inclinations felt. Their generosity may be due to the fact that juries, which—unlike judges in personal injuries cases—do not sit regularly, remember only sensational cases in which sensational awards have been made; alternatively, realisation that a defamation trial provides the media with a second opportunity for publicity may push the jury to be lavish in their awards. Judges, sensitive to the function of the jury in defamation cases, have been unwilling to interfere. *Broome v Cassell* (1972), which confirmed the principle of exemplary damages in libel actions, marked the start of a period of escalating awards. B, a retired naval officer, had been accused in a book published by C of improper conduct and cowardice when in charge of a naval convoy during the Second World War. The jury added £25,000 in exemplary damages to their award of £15,000 in compensatory damages, at the time large sums. Although the House of Lords thought this award excessive, it was not disallowed. The jury was said by Lord Hailsham to be "the only legal and constitutional tribunal for deciding libel cases, including the award of damages" and, so long as "twelve reasonable jurors" could have reached the conclusion, appellate courts should not interfere.

Since then, appellate courts, increasingly aware that relatively minor injury from defamation can result in larger damages than serious personal injury, have interfered more frequently. In *Sutcliffe v Pressdram* (1990), where the wife of a multiple murderer was awarded a huge sum in compensatory damages, an appeal judge pointed out that the investment income on the award would bring in over £1,000 per week. He urged juries, who should know the values "of houses, motorcars, foreign holidays and life insurance policies" to "keep their feet on the ground". In the same year, Parliament intervened. Section 8(2) of the Courts and Legal Services Act 1990 gave appellate courts power to substitute a new award for that of the jury in an appropriate case, obviating the need for an expensive retrial. Exercising its new powers for the first time in *Rantzen v Mirror Group Newspapers* (1993), the Court of Appeal moved towards new guidelines. It cut a jury award of £250,000 to £110,000 and set in place a rudimentary tariff, based on awards previously sanctioned by the Court of Appeal. *John v MGN* (1996)—a bizarre case where Elton John was awarded £275,000 in exemplary damages in respect of an allegation that he had been seen at a party spitting chewed food into a table napkin—provided an opportunity for the Court of Appeal to go further. Judges were urged to give stronger guidance to juries, setting "an appropriate bracket" based on Court of Appeal case law within which awards should be made; the level of damages in personal injuries litigation should also be borne in mind. Exemplary damages should be restricted to cases where the publisher had knowingly or recklessly "peddled untruths", an inference that was not to be lightly drawn. It was, thought Sir Thomas Bingham,

"offensive to public opinion, and rightly so, that a defamation plaintiff should recover damages for injury to reputation greater, perhaps by a significant factor, than if that same plaintiff had been rendered a helpless cripple or an insensate vegetable."

The ratio of costs to damages is frequently disproportionate. The *Reynolds* case was won at trial but the jury expressed its view by awarding 1p in damages. A technical win of this kind endangers the claimant because it exposes him to the risk of having to pay all or part of the defendant's costs. The risk is escalated by statutory provisions, which permit a "payment into court" by a defendant who apologises. In *Reynolds*, therefore, R had to pay the paper's costs from the point at which a payment into court had been made. A summary procedure, introduced by the Defamation Act 1996, slightly ameliorates the position: here a judge sitting alone is authorised to award damages, subject to a maximum of £10,000.

The heavy cost of defamation actions puts pressure on both parties, acting as a deterrent to the publication of controversial material but also precluding action by impecunious members of the public. These weaknesses have landed the United Kingdom before the European Court of Human Rights. The saga of *Aldington v Tolstoy and Watts* (1993) grew out of the strong views held by Count Tolstoy on the conduct of the British Government in returning Cossack refugees to the Soviet forces at the end of the Second World War. T blamed A, then a senior officer in the British army, for the ensuing massacre and his strong feelings unfortunately overflowed into private life, until he circulated a pamphlet defaming A inside Winchester School, where A had become Warden. Although the issue was undoubtedly a matter of public interest, the circulation was not an occasion of qualified privilege. A brought an action to clear his name.

T first applied for the case to be heard by a single judge, on the ground of the complexity of the evidence, but this application failed. His misgivings over jury trial were justified. T was unable to justify the facts on which his comments were based and the jury awarded £1.5 million in damages—surely excessive! A's costs were estimated at £500,000. T appealed. It was calculated that the appeal would last 20 days and cost A an additional £188,000; not unnaturally, A applied for a court order that T should provide "security for costs". T appealed unsuccessfully; the jury verdict stood; and T became bankrupt. By now, the expense of seven hearings, three in the Court of Appeal, of which six were procedural and only one concerned the substance of the libel, were estimated at around £1 million. This sorry situation formed the basis for an application by Count Tolstoy to the European Court of Human Rights. Here T successfully argued that the excessive damages and costs, together with the absence of any right to legal aid, amounted to a violation of his right of free speech under ECHR Art.10 (*Tolstoy Miloslavsky v United Kingdom*, 1995).

Some 10 years later, the point would arise again in the notorious "McLibel case", an action brought by McDonald's against two environmental campaigners, who attacked the environmental impact of the transnational corporation's policies in pamphlets handed out outside its outlets. The trial, before a single judge, took place in 1990 and lasted an awesome 313 days. Because they were not legally aided, the campaigners appeared in person. Neither party won decisively, though McDonald's was awarded £76,000, an award that was never enforced. In the European Court of Human Rights, the "McLibel two" are currently arguing that the massive imbalance in resources made a fair trial impossible; they faced a multinational corporation, which had spent £7 million on their campaign. Their second argument, that a multinational corporation should not have the right to sue in defamation, brings us back to the earlier argument about the importance of free debate on matters of public interest, once more highlighting the freezing effect of defamation on free speech.

PROTECTING PRIVACY

Just as judges are becoming comfortable with the Art.10 "proportionality" formula, the parameters of the debate have changed. Far from unequivocal support for press freedom, there is some public backing today for an extension of tort liability into the new area of privacy. In one of the earliest articles on privacy to be written in this country, Winfield (1931a) defined privacy to mean "a person's seclusion of himself or his property from the public". Tracing privacy through the case law and finding the occasional case in which defamation, trespass to land or private and public nuisance had been useful, Winfield was prepared to deduce the vestiges of such a right. He asked the House of Lords to gather the loose ends together and recognise privacy, like reputation, as an interest worthy of tort law's protection. In taking this line, he was reiterating the argument of a famous American article by Warren and Brandeis (1890). Defining privacy as the individual's "right to be let alone", Warren and Brandeis had demanded that it should be secured.

A modern scholar carrying out Winfield's exercise reiterates his conclusion: defamation and other torts can occasionally be stretched to cover privacy; the case law remains hit and miss (Markesinis, 1990). We too have met such cases, noting their inconsistency. In *Harrison v Duke of Rutland* (1893), trespass on the highway was successfully invoked to protect the Duke's privacy; in *Bernstein v Skyviews* (1978) a similar claim in respect of air space failed. Some defamation cases are best explained in terms of privacy: look back at the bizarre *Khashoggi* case or *John v MGN* and consider the strange case of *Youssopoff v Metro-Goldwyn-Mayer* (1934), where it was held capable of being defamatory to allege that a woman had been raped. In *Khorasandjian* the Court of Appeal was prepared to extend the law of nuisance in the interests of privacy; three years later, in *Hunter v Canary Wharf*, the House of Lords outlawed this development. More recently, in *Wainwright v Home Office* (2003), Lord Hoffmann suggested that one at least of the underlying values protected by the common law and statutory remedies is privacy. Yet, dismissing the "action on the case" in *Wilkinson v Downton* as an aberration "with no leading role in the modern law", Lord Hoffmann emphatically declined to "provide an alternative remedy which distorts the principles of the common law".

Despite momentous technological advances, changes in social circumstances, and changes in the structure and ownership of the media, the legal situation has barely changed since Winfield wrote. Breach of confidence—mentioned in the last chapter as a way to protect commercial secrets—is sometimes capable of protecting privacy and, as with some defamation cases, can give rise to the remedy of injunction. Arguing for a narrowly drawn right of privacy to "strike only at significant infringements", Lord Bingham (1996) has claimed that, in cases where the need to give relief was "obvious and pressing", the courts would not be found wanting. Yet he himself participated in the outrageous case of *Kaye v Robertson* (1990), where a reporter wearing the white coat of a junior doctor gained access to the bedside of a television celebrity hospitalised after a serious accident. K was persuaded, while heavily sedated, to permit photographs to be taken and published. All that the Court of Appeal felt able to do was grant an injunction that authorised the paper to publish the illicit photographs, *provided it was made clear that publication was without consent*. As Markesinis cogently argued, so long as privacy was not in itself recognised as an interest worthy of protection, the law would remain illogical and unsatisfactory. And so it has!

The problem for judicial lawmaking in this area is the diversity of official opinion, coupled with the stated unwillingness of successive governments to take action that might injure press freedom. The Younger Committee, the first of three committees set up by government to make a thorough investigation of the extent to which legal protection ought to be given to personal privacy, thought it a dangerous concept incapable of definition. Younger was absolutely against the imposition of more stringent legal controls on the press, whether by extension of the law of defamation or otherwise; instead, it favoured strengthening the Press Council, which exists to hear complaints from the public about press misconduct, by appointing lay members to represent the public and by giving it adequate regulatory powers (Cmnd.5012, 1972). By the time the Calcutt Committee (Cm.1102, 1990) reported in favour of statutory regulation of the press, the climate had definitely changed. Only the immediate establishment of a voluntary Press Complaints Commission plus a code of practice banning the use of zoom lenses and bugs staved off legislation. But reinstated to assess progress, the Calcutt Committee intensified its demands for a statutory regime (Cm.2135, 1993).

Domestication of the ECHR by the Human Rights Act 1998 left an ambiguous position. The ECHR requires states to provide adequate protection for the right of privacy, balancing the Art.10 right of free speech against the Art.8 right of privacy and giving the two articles equal weight. This is undoubtedly problematic, especially when English judges consistently refuse to acknowledge privacy as a protected interest. In parliamentary debates on the Human Rights Act, it was strenuously argued that Parliament should set out guidelines on the question; this however it declined to do. In *Earl Spencer v United Kingdom* (1998), the Government managed to persuade the Human Rights Commission that privacy could be adequately protected by breach of confidence. This was because the cases had steadily eroded the need for any confidential relationship between the recipient of the confidential information and the person from whom it was obtained. In the later celebrity affair of *Douglas v Hello! Ltd* (2001), the claimants were film stars who, partly in an effort to limit press intrusion into their wedding, had sold the exclusive right to report to *OK!* magazine. *Hello!* magazine circumvented the restriction by publishing unauthorised photographs, smuggled out by a wedding guest. It is very hard to read this, as the courts in fact did, as a breach of confidence, since no relationship existed between the claimants and *OK!*

Refusal to acknowledge a right of privacy and the attempt to base protection on breach of confidence is wrong-footing English courts. As Gault P. trenchantly observed in a similar, New Zealand case:

"Privacy and confidence are different concepts. To press every case calling for a remedy for unwarranted exposure of information about the private lives of individuals into a cause of action having at its foundation trust and confidence will be to confuse these concepts." (*Hosking v Runting*, 2005)

Here the claimant was a television presenter, who asked for an injunction to protect the privacy of his children when photographs taken without the parents' knowledge were to be published in a magazine. By a narrow majority, the New Zealand Court of Appeal decided that the time was ripe for a limited tort of interference with privacy, based on the following criteria:

1. The existence of facts in respect of which there is a reasonable expectation of privacy; and

2. Publicity given to those private facts that would be considered highly offensive to an objective reasonable person.

Applying these markedly restrictive criteria, the court refused the order on the basis that the photographs contained no offensive or seriously intrusive material.

This approach differs strongly from *Campbell v MGN* (2004), where the *Mirror* published photographs of the appellant, a celebrity supermodel, leaving a Narcotics Anonymous meeting. In the House of Lords, the majority started from the premise that *all* the information about Ms Campbell's addiction and attendance at Narcotics Anonymous was both private and confidential, because it had been received from an insider in breach of confidence. Lord Nicholls spoke bravely of human autonomy and dignity:

"I should have thought that the extent to which information about one's state of health, including drug dependency, should be communicated to other people was plainly something which an individual was entitled to decide for herself . . . The whole point of NA is that participants in its meetings are anonymous. It offers them support and the possibility of recovery without requiring them to allow information about their drug dependency to become more widely known."

Yet on the grounds that Ms Campbell was not "an ordinary citizen" but a public figure who had denied being a drug user, the Law Lords thought she had foregone her "reasonable expectation of privacy". Lady Hale too spoke of the risk to the continued success of her treatment, contributing "to the sense of betrayal by someone close to her of which she spoke and which destroyed the value of Narcotics Anonymous as a safe haven for her". Even this did not outweigh the fact that, contrary to previous statements that she had made publicly, Ms Campbell had in fact been involved with illegal drugs.

In *von Hannover v Germany* (2004), the European Court of Human Rights had a turn to consider protection under ECHR Art.8, when Princess Caroline of Monaco-Hanover complained that publication of a series of private photographs breached her right of privacy. The German courts had held that, as a celebrity personality, she had to tolerate photographs taken in public places. The European Court of Human Rights disagreed, holding that the balance between press freedom and privacy had been drawn in the wrong place. Photographs appearing in the tabloid press are, the Court said, often taken in "a climate of continual harassment which induces in the person concerned a very strong sense of intrusion into their private life or even persecution". In situations like the present, where the complainant held no public office and no public or political debate was involved, celebrities enjoy a "legitimate expectation" of respect for their privacy. Privacy must cover all aspects of one's private life, even where these are conducted in public. The decisive factor in balancing press freedom against privacy must be the contribution made by publication to "a debate of general interest".

Experience of defamation shows just how hard it is to draw a line between what is genuinely of public interest and properly the subject of serious investigative journalism and what is—as puritans Warren and Brandeis (1890) put it—simply a trade in "idle gossip", designed to "occupy the indolent" and "satisfy a prurient taste". The press response that celebrities crave the oxygen of publicity is scarcely a persuasive justification of the level of intrusion to which even the general public is increasingly subject. This is a matter of concern to the House of Commons Culture and Media Select Committee. They speak of "media scrums" as a "form of collective harassment" and urge broadcasters, the press industry, and Ofcom, the new broadcasting regulator, "to develop ways of tackling the media scrums that still seem to gather at the scent of a story". They want a new and stiffer Press Complaints Commission and a new twin-track procedure for complainants who want a swift judgment and not mediation. Ultimately, the Committee wants government legislation. But perhaps bearing in mind the heavy costs and trivial nature of many defamation actions, the Report stops short of recommending a new tort of privacy, enforceable in the courts (Select Committee, 2002–03).

When the well-established right to reputation is in question, there is some sense of an appropriate balance between freedom of expression, press freedom and the common law tort of defamation. Where intrusion into privacy is concerned, this is emphatically not the case. Despite the tragedy of Princess Diana, English courts show little sensitivity to the "climate of continual harassment" in which public figures have to live and function. Perhaps a greater failure is blindness to the web of authoritarian state surveillance procedures to which we are all increasingly subject, inside and outside our homes. This type of intrusion into privacy receives only minimal protection through the EU Data Protection Directive (OJ 1995 L281, p.31) and the implementing Data Protection Act 1998. Many years ago, in *Malone v Metropolitan Police Commissioner* (1980), a judge denied a remedy in a case of unauthorised telephone tapping by the police on the ground that no right of privacy existed. Failure adequately to regulate the situation led to a condemnation of the United Kingdom by the European Court of Human Rights (*Malone v United Kingdom*, 1984). More recently, a welcome ruling by that Court establishes that unauthorised publication of an attempted suicide taken by a video camera amounts to a breach of privacy (*Peck v UK*, 2003). Our courts seem perversely blind to the need for protection against these rather more malign types of intrusion into privacy by public officials.

DAMAGES AND THE HUMAN RIGHTS ACT

The obscure and difficult section 8 of the Human Rights Act 1998 raises the question of a wider right to damages. This section allows a court to grant "such relief or remedy . . . within its powers as it considers just and appropriate", though damages may be awarded "only by a court which has power to award damages, or to order the payment of compensation, in civil proceedings", while no award of damages is to be made unless the court is satisfied in all the circumstances that it is necessary to afford "just satisfaction" to the person in whose favour it is made. Courts must, in determining whether to award damages and what the amount of damages should be, "take into account the principles applied by the European Court of Human Rights in relation to the award of compensation under Article 41 of the Convention".

Use of the term "compensation" in these ambiguous provisions could allow courts to treat violations of human rights as falling entirely outside tort law. With the help of the Strasbourg case law, they could then develop special rules for compensation in human rights cases. Alternatively, a special "constitutional tort" could be introduced to cover certain violations of the Human Rights Act, as has been done in some Commonwealth jurisdictions, notably Canada and New Zealand. In both countries this is a fall-back position reserved for exceptional cases and, in England, it was the line of approach that failed in *Marcic* (see above, p.93). A third option is to allow general principles of tort law to govern compensation, a position towards which English courts usually veer.

The European Court of Human Rights has made two efforts to understand the English law of negligence. *Osman v UK* (1998) centred on the signal failure of the police to protect a schoolboy from the harassment of an unbalanced teacher. His conduct culminated in fatal shootings, in which O was seriously injured and his father killed. A civil action in negligence was struck out because the courts held, applying *Hill v Chief Constable of West Yorkshire* (see above, p.42), that it would not be "fair, just and reasonable" to impose a duty of care on the police in respect of the investigation of crime. Blocked in every attempt to secure accountability within the domestic legal system, the lawyers turned to human rights law and took the case to Strasbourg. The European Court of Human Rights ruled that there had been a violation of ECHR Art.6(1), which protects the right of access to a court. By striking out the action, the national courts had deprived the applicant of his right to a judicial hearing; the "fair, just and reasonable" test had operated as "blanket immunity" for the police force. The Court went on to award each of the applicants a sum of £10,000 "on an equitable basis" under Art.41.

The later case of *Z v United Kingdom* (2001) was in the nature of an appeal from *X (Minors) v Bedfordshire* (1995), where, briefly, the right of children to sue a local authority for negligence in the exercise of its statutory child care functions was in issue. (The case is more fully discussed in Ch.8.) The case is normally read as a retraction and something of an apology by the Court, in that it stated clearly that a finding that no duty of care was owed could not be characterised as "either an exclusionary rule or an immunity which deprived [the applicants] of access to court". Again, however, the Court awarded a sum in "just satisfaction" under Art.41.

These influential cases provide a pointer to the thinking of the European Court of Human Rights on damages in human rights cases but they do not go far to resolve problems created by the Human Rights Act. Before the Act came into force, Lord Woolf gave a public lecture arguing that the Act should become "a catalyst for change". But he did not wish to see a "public law damages culture" promoted and took the opportunity to warn against an explosion of damages:

"[T]he days when public bodies could be regarded as having purses of bottomless depth are now past. An award of damages against a Health Authority can reduce the funds resources available for treating patients. An award against a Housing Authority can reduce the funds available for providing or repairing homes." (Woolf, 2000, p.430)

Lord Woolf suggested that damages in human rights cases should be "on the low side with regard to awards in tort cases": no greater sum should be awarded than is necessary to achieve "just satisfaction", with a bar on exemplary or aggravated damages. With human rights litigation on the increase, the time would inevitably come for courts to face the problems of co-ordinating the Act with tort law. It fell to the Court of Appeal to make the attempt in *Anufrijeva v Southwark LBC* (2003). Once again, the case involved the ubiquitous ECHR Art.8. Asylum seekers claimed violations of their right to private and family life in two cases involving delay and maladministration and one based on failure to supply adequate accommodation. In a single judgment delivered by Lord Woolf C.J., the Court of Appeal disallowed the claims. The confusing formula of the Human Rights Act was interpreted to acknowledge "the different role played by damages in human rights litigation to the award of damages in a private law contract or tort action" (Option 1 above). The court drew a bright line between liability in tort and "just satisfaction", where a purely "equitable approach" to compensation is appropriate.

CONCLUSIONS

In the matter of protecting intangible interests, tort law has an uneven record. It has admittedly travelled a long way since the repressive days of criminal libel prosecutions to meet the demands of a society in which freedom of expression is a fundamental democratic value. Some would say that the law has not moved far enough, blaming the freezing effect of defamation actions for a timid and unadventurous press. Press freedom, others would argue, has been taken too far; the balance has slipped from liberty to licence. Tort law has failed to play its proper part in protecting the individual from harassment and the intrusive incursions of the modern media. The State's refusal to intervene cannot excuse the judges for their failure to take privacy seriously. They too must bear responsibility for redressing violations of human rights. Judges, however, have a limited range of remedies at their disposal; all they can do is award damages and the occasional injunction. Opening the door to privacy as a protected interest might replicate the problems of defamation. Perhaps privacy would follow defamation to become an instrument for state officials and the rich and powerful to muzzle the press and cover up their misdeeds.

Even more significant is the issue of damages as a general remedy for human rights violations. This takes us into issues of policy that, as Lord Pearson put it on another occasion (see above, p.21), "raise difficult questions of policy, as well as involving the introduction of new legal principles rather than extension of some principle already recognized and operating".

This type of innovation is not really suitable for judicial decision but needs consideration by the Government and our representatives in Parliament. These are matters for the legislature, which once more has to date stubbornly refused to intervene. Parliament has left to the judges what the judges would prefer to Parliament.

FURTHER READING

Rubinstein gives the flavour of modern defamation cases in *Wicked, Wicked Libels* (London, Routledge & Kegan Paul, 1972). A taste of the very different American law is to be found in Loveland, "Defamation of 'government': Taking Lessons from America?" (1994) 14 *Legal Studies* 206 and "*Reynolds v Times Newspapers* in the House of Lords" [2000] *Public Law* 351. The classic article by Warren and Brandeis is "The Right to Privacy" (1890) 4 *Harvard Law Review* 194. Markesinis has written many articles advocating a right to privacy: see as illustrative "Our Patchy Law of Privacy—Time to do Something About It" (1990) 53 *Modern Law Review* 802. The present state of play is described by Phillipson, "Transforming Breach of Confidence? Towards a Common Law Right of Privacy under the Human Rights Act" (2003) 66 *Modern Law Review* 726. Brownsword presses for a wider role for human dignity in "An Interest in Human Dignity as the Basis for Genomic Torts" [2003] 42 *Washburn Law Journal* 413.

8

SUING THE STATE

DETERRENCE AND ACCOUNTABILITY

The emphasis of earlier chapters of this book was on tort law as *compensation*, a function that we found to depend on liability insurance and vicarious or employers' liability. In this chapter too tort law's compensation function is clearly visible. We shall find litigants attempting to gain access to public funds as an assured source of financial compensation for their losses, a pursuit previously encountered in Ch.6, where we came across several speculative attempts to pass on economic losses. Most public authorities carry liability insurance but this time the ultimate guarantor is the tax fund.

Although we saw that the main thrust of the personal injuries action is compensation, running alongside we found a strong belief in tort law's *deterrent* functions. In Ch.2, we saw that deterrence was a central theme of economic analyses of tort law; the cost of accidents, economists argued, should lie on those best placed to prevent or avoid the harm. In Ch.7, we found that exemplary damages are a regular feature of the defamation action: juries used high awards of damages to punish and deter a damaging and intrusive media, suggesting that the tort action serves purposes other than compensation. In this chapter we shall find tort law's deterrent function again strongly emphasised. We shall find growing use of the tort action for purposes of accountability, as in the Camelford and Hillsborough cases discussed in Ch.2. Tort law's "ombudsman function" seems to be growing in importance and we take up a theme opened up in our earlier discussion of damages in case of human rights violations. In contrast to defamation or privacy actions, human rights cases have to be brought against the state, deemed responsible for permitting a state of affairs in which violations of human rights occur. They too are a factor therefore in creating the "blame culture" and augmenting the volume of litigation against public authorities.

Deterrence and accountability are historic functions of tort law and they lie at the heart of the most famous of all public law liability theories. In lectures published in 1885, Professor A.V. Dicey laid out his rule of law doctrine of "equality before the law". For Dicey, the principle of equality meant primarily that "no man is above the law"; all alike were subject to the ordinary law and amenable to the jurisdiction of the ordinary courts. Proudly, he continued:

"In England the idea of legal equality, or the universal subjection of all classes to one law administered by the ordinary courts, has been pushed to its utmost limit. With us every official, from the Prime Minister down to a constable, is under the same responsibility for every act done without legal justification as any other citizen." (Dicey, 1885, p.187).

Dicey's equality doctrine established two significant points of principle:

- First, that the state in all its manifestations—central, regional and local government, agencies and other public bodies—is subject to the jurisdiction of the "ordinary courts of the land". At the time Dicey wrote, this was not in fact the case. The Crown, though not other public authorities, had just established substantial immunity from liability in tort and contract. This was not ended until the Crown Proceedings Act 1947 was passed, virtually bringing Crown immunity to an end. The Act, which makes the Crown *vicariously* liable for the wrongful acts of public servants, to the same extent as a "person of full age and capacity", reflects Dicey's idea of *personal* liability.

- Secondly, that the principles of liability applicable to state officials are, so far as possible, those applicable to "ordinary" citizens or corporate bodies; state officials are not outside the reach of the principles of the "ordinary" law.

Dicey's model of deterrent justice is seen operating at its best in a set of the eighteenth-century decisions known collectively as the "General Warrant cases" (*Wilkes v Wood*, 1763; *Entick v Carrington*, 1765; *Leach v Money*, 1765). These actions challenged warrants issued by the Home Secretary to search premises, seize property and arrest those engaged in the publication of *The North Briton*, a paper published by John Wilkes, a well-known radical deemed by the authorities to be dangerous. Warrants authorising the search of premises and the seizure of property did not, as they should have done, specifically name the premises to be searched, the property to be seized or the owners. Acting under these warrants, officers entered W's house and that of his printers, seizing their printing press. W and others sued for trespass to goods, and property and false imprisonment, and the courts, in historic judgments, held the officials liable.

A similar landmark is the case of *Cooper v Wandsworth Board of Works* (1863), where C had built some houses for which a licence from the Board of Works was necessary, but had omitted to apply for the licence. As they were apparently entitled to do, the Board of Works demolished the building. When C sued for trespass to land and goods, the court found the Board liable, ruling that a hearing ought to have been granted before the extreme course of demolition was taken. These tort actions were all in the nature of "constitutional torts". They vindicated rights or civil liberties, establishing that, under the common law, government did not possess "police powers" to issue "general warrants" (Jowell, 2000).

The utility of the trespass action in vindicating rights lies in the fact that it requires no proof of damage. It thus throws the burden on officials to show that they are acting within their powers or *intra vires*. If police enter a house to arrest a suspected criminal, they are guilty of trespass unless they can point to some statutory or common law power that justifies their entry; if they mistake the extent of their powers, they become trespassers and may be required to leave. If police search and seize property without legal authority, this is the separate tort of trespass to goods. The same principles apply to other officials who come on to property without the owner's consent: customs officers searching for drugs, tax inspectors looking for VAT returns, gas and electricity board officers to cut off services, or inspectors of the Health and Safety Executive entering a factory to inspect machinery. As Dicey's critics argued, however, there is a serious catch in most of these examples: statute *does* provide "lawful authority" for the trespass. This was not less general when Dicey wrote: police powers were not for example codified until the Police and Criminal Evidence Act 1984, which, with the detailed guidance issued under the Act, catalogues the circumstances in which police powers of arrest, search and seizure may be used.

Dicey's critics were concerned by the growing volume of statutory powers and duties vested in public *officials*. A century later, we live in a regulatory state, in which the powers are vested in the *State*. Public authorities have wide supervisory and regulatory powers and, through its agencies, charged with enforcing standards and protecting the public against risks, the State monitors the performance of public bodies and private enterprise. In this new and somewhat frightening modern world it is public *services* and public *authorities* rather than public *servants* that we want to hold accountable and whose funds we want to access. This trend replicates the trend observed in the law of negligence to replace *personal* liability with an *impersonal* set of non-delegable duties placed upon systems, corporations and corporate bodies (see Ch.2). These are settings in which Dicey's equality doctrine may seem outdated and his ideas questionable.

VINDICATING RIGHTS

In the context of state power, torts that focus on intentional and deliberate wrongdoing have retained an importance long ago ceded elsewhere to negligence. We have met the historic case of *Ashby*, where returning officers in a parliamentary election deliberately refused to allow two of the registered electors to vote. Like *Wilkinson*, which it resembles, *Ashby* is one of the anomalous "actions on the case" met from time to time throughout this book, where a judge wants to award damages for a wrong that does not precisely fit the scheme of tort law. Today, we would probably categorise the *Ashby* principle, where the returning officers' action was described as an "excessive and insolent use of power", as a "misfeasance in public office". This anomalous nominate tort provides redress for the misuse of power by public officials. Once more we find that the criteria for liability remain uncertain and that the parameters of the tort—despite attempts by the courts to define the tort and map its boundaries—are far from clear. In *Three Rivers DC v Bank of England* (2000), briefly discussed in the context of economic loss, the courts took much time and trouble to establish a set of constituent elements for the previously inchoate cause of action. As summarised by Fairgrieve (2002, pp.86–95), the criteria are that:

- the defendant must be a public official;

- the act complained of must be an exercise of public power;

- damage must be suffered;

- the official must have acted maliciously or recklessly.

This is relatively simple where the claimant can either prove bad faith or "targeted malice", in the sense of intention to cause harm to the particular claimant. This was the situation in *Kuddus v CC of Leicestershire Constabulary* (2001), where a police officer investigating a theft took it upon himself to cancel the complaint without the complainant's consent, forging his signature to do so. It is less clear what the position is if the defendant showed "reckless indifference" to the question of legality. Malice is a slippery term and one which allows for slippage first from a subjective to an objective test of intention; thence from reckless indifference to gross negligence; and thence to negligence pure and simple.

In *Rookes v Barnard* (1964), when Lord Devlin retained abuse of public power a ground for the award of exemplary damages, he drew on the "General Warrant cases". In *Ashby* it was said that "if *public officers* will infringe men's rights, they ought to pay greater damages than other men to deter and hinder others from the like offences". In *Rookes* too, the House of Lords agreed that exemplary damages were appropriate to "vindicate the strength of the law" in cases of oppressive, arbitrary or unconstitutional action by public servants: "the servants of the government are also the servants of the people and the use of their power must always be subordinate to their duty of service". The common law follows public opinion in allowing exemplary and punitive damages to be awarded in a tort action, and there is now vicarious liability for such awards (*Kuddus*, above). This is a matter of some importance as, when a jury tries actions against the police, very large sums may be awarded.

"Aggravated damages" may, according to the Law Commission, be awarded in preference to exemplary or punitive damages to mark the affront to dignity from insult or humiliation while preserving the modern view of tort law as purely compensatory (Law Com.1997, p.10). In one fairly typical case, where a Sunday school teacher brought a successful action for assault, false imprisonment and malicious prosecution against the police, a jury awarded £26,000 for the added humiliation that the police had looked under her skirt. Doubt was, however, cast on awards of this type when the courts stepped in—as they had done with defamation damages—to regulate and limit jury awards. These were seen once more to be out of line with damages in personal injuries cases (*Thompson v MPC*, 1997). Judges were advised to instruct juries carefully and to divide awards into two parts: "basic" and "aggravated" damages. Aggravated damages would be appropriate only where they amounted to more than £1,000 and they should not add up to more than twice the basic award. Exemplary damages would be inappropriate unless an award of £5,000 or more was contemplated to mark the jury's disapproval of oppressive or arbitrary behaviour; even then conduct must be particularly deserving of condemnation and involve senior officers to merit awards of over £25,000. It seems unlikely that the general public appreciates these fine distinctions; the ostensibly punitive nature of the tort action, recognised in the right to exemplary and aggravated damages, is one reason why it is so attractive as a means of exacting accountability.

Two centuries after the "General Warrant cases" and one century after Dicey wrote, tort law still occasionally fulfils its function in checking abuses of public power. New causes of action based on human rights violations offer an opportunity to the judiciary to refurbish the police torts. Yet this is a course of action they seem unwilling to take. Turn back to *Wainwright* (see above, p.16), where a mother and son were visiting a relative detained in prison under suspicion of being a drug dealer, and stripsearching was ordered. The claimants sued in traditional fashion for assault and battery, arguing that, although the prison officers honestly believed that they had a right under the rules to stripsearch the Wainwrights and had not intended to cause distress nor realised that they were acting unlawfully, they had not kept within the terms of r.86(1) of the Prison Rules 1964. The House of Lords ruled in favour of the son, where the stripsearch involved physical contact of a kind not "generally acceptable in the ordinary conduct of daily life"; in the mother's case, however, there had been no touching, hence no trespass. The House of Lords could not be persuaded that stripsearching exceeded what is "necessary and proportionate" to deal with the serious drug smuggling problem in prisons and refused to expand the boundaries of tort law to cover a case where, even if human dignity was in issue, no lasting injury could be shown.

CREEPING NEGLIGENCE AGAIN

The theme of this book has been the creeping growth of negligence and, in Ch.3, we saw how the *Dorset Yacht* case opened the way for negligence actions against central government. Alongside, we have tracked the trend to pin liability on well-funded corporate defendants and insurers. The State has the deepest pockets: while local government and other public authorities insure, central government draws on the tax fund, setting the State in place as a target for litigants. But judges hesitate to impose civil liability, reasoning either that public servants might be inhibited from using statutory powers given by Parliament for public purposes or that the tax fund should not be used for the award of damages. Times change. In the *Dorset Yacht* case, Lord Reid forcefully expressed his conviction that public servants are made of "stern stuff"; later, we find it said in *Yuen Kun-yeu* that public servants, who "apply their best endeavours" to the performance of their public duty, should not be discouraged from carrying out their functions for fear of inculcating "a detrimentally defensive frame of mind". Both views are apparent in the modern case law, together with a great unwillingness, in the absence of express parliamentary authorisation, to burden the taxpayer with liability for losses caused by the exercise of statutory functions. While courts are generally happy to draw the inference that liability is intended from industrial safety legislation, they are much less willing to treat statutes such as the Housing (Homeless Persons) Act 1977, which imposes duties on local authorities to rehouse the homeless, or the Education Acts 1944 and 1988, in the same way. These are likely to be read as creating "public" duties, owed to the public at large and not to individuals, the proper mode of enforcement being an application for judicial review. Again, the claimant must fall within the "class of person for whose benefit the statute was intended"; thus building regulations are intended to promote safety and the courts will not construe them to benefit someone who suffers purely economic loss (*Governors of the Peabody Donation Fund v Sir Lindsay Parkinson*, 1985). In this way, zip fasteners have been attached to the "deep pockets" of public bodies.

The waters are muddied by conceptual confusion over the nature of statutory powers and duties: *duties* are mandatory; *powers* imply discretion, though this should not mean that a *common law* duty cannot be bolted on to statutory *power*. In *Anns*, a local authority surveyor acting under statutory powers to inspect buildings had either decided not to inspect the foundations of a block of flats or else had made a negligent inspection. The House of Lords tried to resolve the problem of discretion by introducing a distinction between a protected "policy" area of decision-making and the "operational" acts by which policies and decisions are carried out. But this has not proved decisive.

The entrenched common law distinction between a wrongful act (misfeasance) and omission to act (nonfeasance) makes everything harder. In *Stovin v Wise* (1996), a traffic accident occurred when a driver turned negligently out of a blind junction, previously identified by the highway authority as an accident black spot. Norfolk County Council as highway authority had contacted British Rail, the landowner, for permission to carry out modifications, but subsequently failed to notice that no reply had been received and to follow the matter up. This was clearly an operational error. The Law Lords were nonetheless uncomfortable: they saw an obvious problem with causation in that, if a lawful decision *not* to take action had been taken, the accident would still have occurred. Speaking for the majority, Lord Hoffmann simply discarded the inconvenient policy/operational distinction as "an inadequate tool", arguing that, even if a clearly operational error were found, it did not necessarily follow that liability should be imposed, while Lord Nicholls overrode the power/duty problem by saying that the council had "failed to fulfil its public law obligations just as much as if it were in breach of a statutory duty". Eight years later, the House of Lords found it necessary to return to the problem in a second tragic road accident case (*Gorringe v Calderdale MBC*, 2004). A mother had driven her car head-on into a bus on a country road, severely injuring herself and killing her daughter and her young friend. She argued that a crest in the road of which no warning was given had created the illusion that the bus, which was properly driven, was on her side. On the face of things, the accident was the fault of the car driver: "but for" her mistake, the accident would not have occurred. A claim was nonetheless made against the council, as responsible for failing to give proper warning. Disposing trenchantly of the claim, Lord Hoffmann tried to close the door to similar cases, saying that he found it

"difficult to imagine a case in which a common law duty can be founded simply upon the failure (however irrational) to provide some benefit which a public authority has power (or a public law duty) to provide."

This echoes his remarks in *O'Rourke v Camden LBC* (1997), where the claimant had been wrongfully evicted from temporary accommodation pending a final decision on his entitlement to public housing. The House of Lords ruled against liability, with Lord Hoffmann invoking the "collective interest" to deduce that

Parliament did not intend "cash payments to be made by way of damages to persons who, in breach of the housing authority's statutory duty, have unfortunately not received the benefits which they should have done".

X (Minors) v Bedfordshire County Council (1995) represents a previous effort by the House of Lords finally to dispose of the issue of liability for loss caused by statutory powers and duties. Two sets of joined cases were before the House of Lords. The first set tested the liability of local education authorities for systemic failures to diagnose and deal with the special educational needs of children. In the educational cases, the House of Lords thought liability possible, since the duty of care was well-established and did not derive from statute; perhaps they were only saying that, since medical personnel were liable whether they worked in the private or public sector, this should apply to psychiatrists working for an education authority. Speaking for the House, Lord Browne-Wilkinson asserted that it was neither helpful nor necessary "to introduce public law concepts as to the *validity* of a decision into the question of *liability* at common law for negligence". A minor flood of actions followed this ruling. In *Phelps v Hillingdon Borough Council* (2001), for example, the local education authority had employed an educational psychologist to diagnose learning difficulties. She negligently failed to diagnose dyslexia and in consequence, it was argued, a pupil left school with fewer skills than if she had been diagnosed earlier. In this case, the Law Lords saw no good reason for "treating work in the classroom as territory which the courts must never enter". Undeterred by fears of "gold-digging actions", they went on to hold that there was no overriding reason why someone employed by a local education authority to carry out professional services should not in principle owe a duty of care to particular pupils.

The second set of cases in *X v Bedfordshire* dealt with the potential liability of social workers exercising statutory powers designed for the protection of children under a series of Children Acts, a situation without a private law parallel. These, the House concluded, failed the "fair, just and reasonable" test of negligence on policy grounds. As we saw in the last chapter, this ruling resulted in a dispute with the European Court of Human Rights, resolved in *Z v United Kingdom* (see above, p.136). Subsequently, the possibility of damages in actions in respect of powers under the Children Acts was tested and retested until, in *JD v East Berkshire* (2003) the Court of Appeal ruled that *X v Bedfordshire* could not survive the Human Rights Act. It will no longer be legitimate to rule as a matter of law that no duty of care is owed to a child the subject of a suspected child abuse because each case will fall to be decided on its individual facts—a most unsatisfactory position.

TOWARDS A PUBLIC LAW OF LIABILITY?

The disparities we have seen in this chapter have led some writers to argue for a specialised *public* law of tort to take account of "the particular economic environment within which public bureaucracies operate" (Cohen, 1993). A public law variant of theories of enterprise liability (see above, pp.30–37) might suggest that the State, which is acting in the public interest when it invokes statutory powers, should also bear any losses caused. It is sometimes also argued—though not usually by economic analysts—that this is an efficient method of risk allocation because the costs can be widely spread through the tax fund. Similarly, a general principle of compensation could be propounded according to which the risk of *all* illegality should fall on the State and not the citizen (Cane, 1999). Neither theory is likely to recommend itself to British judges, notably sparing with public funds; they are more likely to take the view that the "deep pockets" of government should not be treated as a free and bottomless insurance fund.

The only significant step towards a public law principle of liability has been taken under the influence of the European Court of Justice (ECJ), whose case law, in contrast to that of the European Court of Human Rights discussed in the last chapter, is more than an influence on English law: it has to be obeyed. In the fields in which the European Union has competence, its legal system constitutes a superior legal order and the judgments of the European Court of Justice are binding on British courts. We have already noted the *Milk Marketing Board* case (see above, p.105), where violation of the EC Treaty was held to be a breach of statutory duty. In *Francovich v Italy* (1991), the ECJ held that failure to transpose an EU directive was a breach of EU law, giving rise to liability, setting out the three following criteria:

- the directive must be intended to confer rights on individuals;

- the content of the rights must be clearly spelt out in the directive;

- there must be a causal link between the failure to implement the directive and the loss suffered.

The *Factortame* case established that, when EU law is in question, the State can be held liable for economic losses, even where it is acting in a legislative capacity and in the absence of fault. The United Kingdom had violated EU fisheries policy, incorrectly transposed by the Merchant Shipping Act 1988. Fishermen put out of business by the legislation and concurrent regulations brought actions claiming compensation for economic loss. On a reference to the Court of Justice, the *Francovich* principle was pared down to situations where the breach of EU law was "sufficiently serious" or "manifest and grave" (*Brasserie du Pêcheur and Factortame*, 1996). This was not enough to protect the British Government. In *Factortame No 5* (1999), the House of Lords ruled that the legislation did contain a manifest and grave error of transposition. Whether a new Eurotort has been established or whether, as Lord Woolf hinted in *Anufrijeva* (see above, p.136), there is simply a right to compensation remains to be seen (Craig, 1993).

CONCLUSIONS

Today, when tort law's accountability function has been partially superseded by the growth of a complex system of administrative law remedies, judicial review has become the standard way to challenge the legality of administrative action. Real ombudsmen have replaced tort law, rendering the notion of "tort law as ombudsman" less attractive. We should bear in mind, however, that alternative remedies are sometimes illusory: the police complaints system established by the Police Act 1976 as a substitute for the expensive and lengthy civil action is an example: it does not, as it probably should, provide for compensation, so that it drives claimants back towards the tort system. On some occasions again, the courts have to recognise the compelling demands of corrective justice and the overriding rule of law principle that wrongs must be redressed. Dicey's equality principle still reflects "a widely-held political ideal" and to abandon it would be read as a serious dilution of accountability to the courts (Hogg, 1989, p.2). This argument is, however, weakened by the many occasions on which the courts, as they did in *Wainwright*, refuse to respond, and their—perhaps temporary—reluctance to draw on the Human Rights Act for assistance and support.

More justified is the protective attitude that has grown up with regard to public funds. *O'Rourke* is only one of the cases which have made the judicial concern about resources clear. Lord

Hoffmann echoes the sentiments of Lord Woolf, cited in the context of the Human Rights Act. The judges have always been concerned to maintain the "floodgates". They do not wish to contribute to the creation of a society bent on litigation, premised on the illusion that every misfortune merits compensation. Even if there is little concrete evidence to justify fear of a "compensation culture", we can see that many modern cases are class actions or test cases, like the *Bedfordshire* cases (see above p.147), with serious implications for public funds. The sums in issue are often very large and one success in court inevitably generates further claims.

The mystery is why resources and insurance are shrugged aside on some occasions when on others they seem to be decisive. Housing is a social service and so is childcare but so too is education. All three services are funded from taxation and administered by local authorities. Children are "vulnerable victims" but so are the homeless. If, as Lord Hoffmann so energetically asserts, liability to a homeless person cannot be based on "failure (however irrational) to provide some benefit which a public authority has power (or a public law duty) to provide", why is this somehow different if the victim is a dyslexic child? The unpredictable outcomes of a conceptually weak case law make it hard for public authorities to understand their obligations and calculate their possible liabilities.

Like economic loss, negligent or technically illegal administrative action creates a risk of "liability in an indeterminate amount for an indeterminate time to an indeterminate class". Moreover, the bipolar nature of the tort action means that the wider implications of the cases may be hidden. There is an argument that the Government, which administers the tax fund, is better placed than a court to decide which risks it will underwrite through *ex gratia* payments and administrative compensation schemes. We shall examine this argument in the final chapter.

FURTHER READING

Many of the ideas in this chapter are developed in Harlow, *State Liability: Beyond Tort Law* (Oxford, Oxford University Press, 2004). Linden advances the case for tort damages in public law cases in "Tort Law as Ombudsman" (1973) 51 *Canadian Bar Review* 155. This exposition, which has never been bettered, is reassessed in Linden, "Reconsidering Tort Law as Ombudsman", in F.M. Steel and S. Rodgers-Magnet, *Issues in Tort Law* (Toronto, Carswell,

1983). The evolution of public authority liability is covered by Craig, "Negligence in the Exercise of a Statutory Power" (1978) 94 *Law Quarterly Review* 428 and the more recent case law by Craig and Fairgrieve, "*Barrett*, Negligence and Discretionary Powers" [1999] *Public Law* 626. On misfeasance, see Evans, "Damages for Unlawful Administrative Action: The Remedy for Misfeasance in Public Office" (1982) 31 *International and Comparative Law Quarterly* 640, or Andenas and Fairgrieve, "Misfeasance in Public Office, Governmental Liability and European Influences" (2002) 51 *International and Comparative Law Quarterly* 757. For an introduction to EU law on Member State liability, start with Ross, "After Francovitch" (1993) 56 *Modern Law Review* 55.

9

THE FUTURE OF TORT

TORT LAW IN CRISIS?

Over the last quarter-century several of tort law's most distinguished scholars have talked of its future in pessimistic terms. There was much disappointment in Britain when the 1978 Report from the Pearson Commission on personal injuries litigation was pigeonholed; commentators were not entirely uncritical (Allen, Bourne and Holyoak, 1979) but some action was surely necessary. In the 1980s, both Fleming (1984) and Atiyah (1987a) were asking whether tort law had a future. In 2003, Deakin, Johnston and Markesinis described tort law as "at a crossroads", where it has incidentally remained since their last edition. There is similar concern in the United States, where Fleming concluded his study of the American tort process (Fleming, 1987, p.265) by saying:

"Even the substantive tort law is unequal to dealing fairly and effectively with systematic problems of causation in mass accident and mass exposure cases. To the extent that traditional rules are already being modified in order to facilitate recovery by victims, the tort system is being distorted, even superseded. If the conventional tort law is thus proving itself inadequate to the task, should we not, instead of merely tinkering with it, consider the more radical solution of entirely replacing it?"

Fleming lived through tort law's growth period during the 1960s and 1970s, a period described by Schwartz (1992) as a period of "plaintiff's greatest hits". He had watched the rise of mass tort litigation (Rosenberg, 1984). The "Agent Orange case" brought against the United States Government in respect of defoliants used in Vietnam had involved millions of claims (Schuck, 1986). He had watched again as the class action pioneered in the United States began to assume global dimensions, starting with transnational products liability litigation against multinational corporations. Today, the sums claimed in transnational litigation that routinely crosses national boundaries and defies time limits are enormous, able to drive corporate defendants and their insurers into bankruptcy. Around 500,000 asbestos workers and their families have sued over a period of 40 years in the United States alone in respect of asbestosis, and it is estimated that claims may peak at two million before the crisis ends. American juries have gone wild, in one case awarding $55.5 million to a single family. Insurers have paid out more than $20 billion and the final estimate is around $200 billion. British insurers expect claims in the region of £6–8 billion. Three Supreme Court judges have given their opinion that "a nationwide administrative claims processing regime would provide the most secure, fair, and efficient means of compensating victims of asbestos" and that legislation was needed to deal with "the elephantine mass of asbestos cases" (*Amchem Products v Windsor*, 1997, Ginsburg J; *Ortiz v Fibreboard Corporation*, 1999, Souter and Rehnquist JJ.). As more and more companies with less and less connection to asbestos production have been drawn into the litigation, at least five bankruptcy petitions, with 17 more in the offing, have been filed. Stock prices have dropped and access to capital for companies involved has diminished. Notably, it is estimated that successful claimants in these cases have received less than 40 per cent of damages awarded, while the sums paid out to lawyers have absorbed a large share (Hensler, 2002; Isscharoff, 2002).

These facts and figures help to explain why Huber (1988, pp.4, 164) talks of tort law in terms of a "tort tax", which puts

"a damper on communal enterprise . . . When all is said and done, the modern rules do not deter risk, they deter behaviour that gets people sued, which is not at all the same thing. The most innovative and most easily curtailed go."

He is not alone. Ten years later and Huber's analysis was mirrored in Australia. Spigelman J., the present Chief Justice of New South Wales, spoke of an "element of welfare state paternalism" in judicial thinking that drove "day-to-day judicial decision making about when a person ought to receive compensation" (Spigelman, 2002; 2004). A "vulnerable victim" attitude to compensation in the courts was feeding a growing "compensation culture", or vice versa—the influences were no doubt circular (Luntz, 1996; 1998). In any event, there were dramatic changes in the law of negligence, to which the legislature had reacted with a substantial package of reforms. We shall return to this in due course.

Let us first return for a moment to the Pearson Commission, which sat for five years and reported after commissioning many studies and taking evidence from a wide range of experts (Cmnd.7054, 1978). Although the Report was never implemented, it remains the most complete source of information and ideas about the English tort system. Statistics presented to the Commission made one point abundantly clear: tort law was not the major source of accident compensation in the United Kingdom. Each year there were over three million injuries serious enough to lead to four or more days' absence from work, of which 21,000 were fatal. Of these about 720,000 occurred at the work-place and 290,000 involved traffic accidents. Of the remaining accidents, about one million occurred in the home and generally fell outside the tort system altogether. There were about 250,000 tort claims in respect of personal injury annually, of which 85–90 per cent were either wholly or partially successful; 86 per cent were resolved without the necessity for legal action and *only 1 per cent reached the courts*. But this apparently high success rate was insignificant in comparison to the total number of accidents; it amounted to only 6.5 per cent of accidents suffered.

Some more recent facts and figures help us to update this snap-shot of personal injuries litigation in the 1970s. Data from the NHS body set up specifically to deal with litigation showed that NHS expenditure on clinical negligence has risen from £1 million (evaluated as the equivalent of £6.33 million in today's prices) in 1974–75 (around the time of Pearson) to £446 million in 2001–02. The legal and administrative costs of settling claims exceeded the money actually paid to victims. A recent report from the National Audit Office (2002–03) revealed that £100 million was paid out by the Ministry of Defence in the year 2002–03 to servicemen and women injured through negligence, a four-fold increase over 10 years. Further claims of "hundreds of millions of pounds", which include the disputed Gulf War veterans' claim, the subject of a major class action, were in the pipeline. The Institute of Actuaries announced recently that the cost of compensation in civil actions in the United Kingdom has risen to £10 billion annually, amounting to 1 per cent of GDP! Of this enormous sum, £2 billion goes to lawyers.

TORT LAW AS ACCIDENT COMPENSATION

A survey of 1,711 accident victims carried out by the Oxford Centre for Socio-Legal Studies (the Oxford Survey) also found low success rates for accident victims: only 12 per cent of the victims obtained damages through the tort system; of the rest, 85 per cent made no claim and 2 per cent made a claim which was later abandoned. The survey called the tort action

"a compulsory long-distance obstacle race. The victims, without their consent, are placed at the starting line, and told that if they complete the whole course, the umpire at the finishing line will compel the race-promoters to give them a prize; the amount of the prize, however, must remain uncertain until the last moment because the umpire has discretion to fix it individually for each finisher. None of the runners is told the distance he must cover to complete the course; nor the time it is likely to take. Some of the obstacles in the race are fixed hurdles (rules of law), while others can, without warning, be thrown into the path of a runner by the race-promoters, who obviously have every incentive to restrict the number of runners who can complete the course . . . In view of all the uncertainties, and particularly the difficulties which could be presented by the unknown, future obstacles, many runners drop out of the race at each obstacle . . . and most runners accept an offer and retire. The few hardy ones who actually finish may still be disappointed with the prize money." (Harris, 1984, pp.132–33)

Harris's first hurdle is the proof of negligence, which can be very difficult. The victim of a serious road accident is not in a position to go round collecting names and addresses; professional people stand together, as do members of any big organisation, and may refuse to give evidence against one another; it may be hard to get access to vital documents, such as medical or police records. The Oxford Survey found many complaints about both solicitors and trade unions in handling litigation and negotiating and settling claims, especially in respect of delay and cost. The burden of proof remains a heavy one, nowhere more so than in the medical cases discussed in Ch.4. The scene of a factory accident is wholly in the control of the employer and manufacturing processes are closely guarded secrets, making it hard to show negligence. Sometimes a court may "presume negligence", as in *Grant v Australian Knitting Mills* (1936), where G sued for damages after contracting a skin disease from underclothes shown to contain sulphite, an irritant chemical. Although the mill was able to show that its manufacturing system was virtually foolproof, the Privy Council rejected its defence, holding it liable in the absence of any exact explanation. In that case the court reached a decision consonant with a standard of strict liability within the framework of negligence.

In other cases, judges have shown themselves willing to lighten the burden of proving causation: compare *Grant* with the decision in *McGhee*. But even if claimants can leap the hurdle of causation, the race has not yet been won. Nothing is harder to forecast than the way in which tort damages will be assessed. The traditional lump sum awards (see below) entail guesswork about rates of inflation, tax, and interest return on capital, as well as more critical factors, like changes in the victim's medical condition and his probable length of life. Claimants may also bump into the contributory negligence doctrine (see above, p.62), which deprives them of part of their prize. Finally, the "conditional fee" system, used nowadays to finance many personal injuries actions, often allows the lawyers to take a substantial share of damages awarded, unless insured against (*Callery v Gray*, 2002).

Fortunately for accident victims, they do not all have to embark on the obstacle race. As the Oxford Survey showed, alternative and more convenient sources of accident compensation exist. Of these, the most significant is the social security system, which provides a variety of contributory and non-contributory, means-tested and non-means-tested benefits including sickness benefit, industrial injuries compensation and income support. The industrial injuries scheme is also a significant source of compensation. First-party insurance and pensions schemes also often help.

In his masterly exposition of the subject, Atiyah (1970) advocated remodelling the social security system to cover compensation for all injury, work-caused illness and disability. Distinctions based on causation would disappear; all the disabled and all invalids would be entitled to benefits calculated on the basis of their degree of invalidity and paid periodically on a weekly or monthly basis. The only national accident compensation scheme is, however, that set up in New Zealand, following the 1967 Woodhouse Royal Commission (Harris, 1974). This handles claims from anyone who suffers a "personal injury by accident" or from his or her dependants in case of death. Lump sum payments are made, based on the rates of damages at common law, and these are broadly related to earnings. Claims to the fund are dealt with by administrative procedures very like those of our own Criminal Injuries Compensation Board (see below); they are administered by the Accident Compensation Corporation and partly financed by contributions from employers, employees, car owners and the medical profession. Widely praised as effective, cheap and efficient, though also criticised as rather inflexible and bureaucratic, the New Zealand scheme forms a prototype for other systems. All actions for damages in respect of personal injury or death have been abolished; in New Zealand, tort law is virtually dead.

Introduced in 1964, the British Criminal Injuries Compensation Scheme (CICS) is a "no fault" compensation scheme, operating outside the legal system but until recently pegged in principle to damages in tort law. The CICS has been the object of very wide take-up, with a consistent escalation both in claims and also in the awards paid out in compensation. In the first 30 years of its lifespan, the Board handled 730,420 applications and paid out £909,446,123 in compensation, and nearly three-quarters of the applications were successful. Consequently, costs leapt from £33,430 in 1964 to £109 million in 1992–3, when the Conservative Government moved to a "banded tariff" scheme, which was introduced by the Criminal Injuries Compensation Act 1995 (Duff, 1998).

The way this change was effected marks an important distinction between the independent tort law system and a compensation scheme, funded and operated by and wholly within the control of the Government. Accident compensation does not, like the tort system, treat the victim individually and aim to make his losses "whole". The revised scheme caps claims at a maximum of £500,000 for all but a tiny minority of severely injured victims and imposes a minimum threshold, with a view to excluding trivial claims. It has 25 bands, capped at £250,000 for the most serious categories of injury, and a threshold of £1,000 below which compensation is not claimable. While tort law tends to offer "golden handshakes" to the most seriously injured, accident compensation advantages the less seriously hurt. This is one reason why claims to accident compensation schemes grow exponentially, a characteristic of both the New Zealand and British schemes, justifying the threshold and casting light too on the escalation of tort litigation described above. Perhaps we are really in the grip of a compensation culture, targeted at any or every source of financial compensation.

Although the Oxford Survey showed most tort awards to be relatively small, damages in case of serious injury can be very large indeed, reflecting the escalating cost of technological development in health care. In *Wells v Wells* (1998), the House of Lords had the opportunity of considering the scale of damages, at a time when the Law Commission was engaged in a full and thorough survey of damages in tort law. The House considered three cases, in all of which the damages hovered around the £1 million mark: a 60-year-old part-time nurse who had suffered serious brain damage in a car accident and was awarded a sum of £1,619,332 on a life expectancy of 15 years; a baby with cerebral palsy due to birth injuries, who was awarded £1,307,963; and a 24-year-old worker severely injured in an industrial accident, who received £997,345. All three awards had been reduced by the Court of Appeal. The House of Lords scrutinised the methods used to calculate the damages, based on a rather different tariff system to that of the CICS, with actuarial tables as its starting point. They then unanimously restored the awards of the trial judges. It is hard to see a compensation plan competing with these high awards. Rates are moreover rising. In *Heil v Rankin* (2000), a specially convened panel of Court of Appeal judges announced increases in awards for pain and suffering and loss of amenity, often the most substantial element in serious accident cases. Awards under these headings are in practice largely notional; as Atiyah once put it (Cane, 1999, p.83), they could be "multiplied or divided by two overnight and they would be just as defensible or indefensible as they are today". This is effectively what was done in *Heil*, although, even then, the Court of Appeal did not go so far in uprating as the Law Commission wished to go (Law Com.257, 1999).

In reality, it has to be admitted that all awards of damages are really rather speculative, as the judge knows neither precisely how long the victim will live nor how long he would have worked in the normal course of events nor what the costs of future care and future loss of earnings will be. To deal with this problem, tort damages, traditionally payable in a single lump sum, which can be invested, are increasingly paid in "periodical payments", authorised by the Damages Act 1996. Courts are asked to approve a "structured settlement", popular with insurers called upon to meet very large awards, or a lump sum can be combined with one or more annuities, guaranteed for life or for a fixed term and index-linked to combat inflation (Lewis, 1993, pp.847–848).

Let us apply this information to the case of medical negligence, shown in previous chapters to be a growth area of negligence, with many problems of proof and evidence. It is fair to say that in no other area of personal injuries law is a compensation plan more necessary. Yet fear of escalating claims is a serious deterrent to introducing such a plan in medical cases. Since 2001, the options for reform have been under consideration by the

Department of Health, and a report from the Chief Medical Officer has now been issued (Donaldson, 2003, p.7). The conclusion of the review group with regard to clinical negligence actions was that:

"Legal proceedings for medical injury frequently progress in an atmosphere of confrontation, acrimony, misunderstanding and bitterness. The emphasis is on revealing as little as possible about what went wrong, defending clinical decisions that were taken and only reluctantly releasing information. In the past, cases have taken too long to settle. In smaller value claims the legal costs have been disproportionate to the damages awarded. In larger value claims there can be lengthy and expensive disputes about the component parts of any lump sum payment and the anticipated life span of the victim."

It is, then, surprising to find the Chief Medical Officer's review *rejecting* the strong case for no-fault compensation in cases of medical misadventure largely because of fear of escalating claims. The harmful consequences of health care were found to be much greater than had been previously recognised: the review found that perhaps 10 per cent of hospital in-patients report adverse effects from hospitalisation, with 5 per cent of the population reporting adverse effects of medical care. If we feed in the information that accident compensation tends to advantage the less seriously hurt, it is easy to see why the review feared a cost escalation: they estimated that compensation payments might reach a sum as high as £4 billion. To be affordable, compensation would need to be set at a substantially lower level than current tort awards and this would inevitably disadvantage seriously injured victims. They could, of course, be excluded from the scheme, preserving for them the "golden handshake" of tort law. There would, however, be something of an irony in leaving only the most seriously injured victims to jump the hurdles of the "obstacle race".

The case against tort law as a vehicle for accident compensation, most powerfully advanced by the New Zealand Woodhouse Report (1967) and Atiyah (1970) is strong and certainly receives support from the available empirical studies. Remember the Ontario studies that set out to test evidence on the efficacy of the torts system and alternatives in cases of traffic accident, medical misadventure, products liability, industrial accident and environmental damage (see above, pp.40–41). The authors concluded that "the deterrent properties of the tort system seem strongest for auto accidents and weakest for environmentally related accidents. The incentive effects of the system are mixed in the case of medical and product-related accidents, making net welfare judgments problematic; in the case of workplace accidents, workers' compensation levies appear to have stronger deterrent effects than the tort system did have or might have if it were resurrected in this context. From a compensation perspective, the tort system appears to fail badly in all five areas, with the failure being most severe for environmentally related, product-related, and medically induced injuries. In a corrective justice perspective, the tort system appears to perform reasonably well for automobile accidents but much less well for medically induced and environmentally-related injuries; its performance for product-related accidents is unclear." (Dewes, Duff and Trebilcock, 1996 p.v)

But experience of administrative compensation plans in operation show that they do not have all the advantages claimed for them. They do not always succeed indeed in ironing out disputes over proof. The arguments are simply transferred from the terrain of fault to the equally difficult terrain of causation. For the same reason that strict liability does not always produce a better result for the claimant than negligence (Newdick, 1985), compensation plans often fail to compensate victims. The no-fault Vaccine Damage Compensation Scheme set up in Britain with the objective of persuading parents to have their children immunised largely failed: proof of negligence was not the issue, but inability to establish causation (Dworkin, 1979). There is a warning too in the meagre benefits provided by our existing social security system. These hardly amount to a "golden handshake", while the experience of those who have to operate the system is—to borrow a phrase used earlier of tort law—"the underlying callousness of its ideology". To replace tort by a welfare benefits system may be only to exchange the problems of a private lawyer for those of a public lawyer.

Finally, as we saw in Ch.2, the tort action has benefits other than compensation. The accident compensation plan has consistently met fairly heavy criticism in New Zealand for its allegedly detrimental effect on health and safety and accident prevention—allegations of which there is no proof. For similar reasons, medical misadventure cases are under scrutiny in New Zealand, where a handful of cases publicised as unsatisfactory has led to demands for reinstatement of the right to sue. The motivation for

Bottrill v A (see above, p.43), where the claimant used a claim for exemplary damages to circumvent the ouster clause of the Accident Compensation Acts, was a desire for accountability (Ferguson, 2003). Klar (1983), a strong opponent of the abolition of tort law, argues that accident compensation ignores the features of deterrence, accountability and culpability provided by the tort action and thus provides "free insurance for wrongdoers". We find the free insurance argument advanced about criminal injuries compensation in Britain, though the present power of the victims' lobby has so far been able to fend off serious incursions into the scheme. All the arguments about tort law's underlying objectives outlined in Ch.2 are being reintroduced.

PRAGMATISM AND PRINCIPLE

None of this is enough to dispose of the set of theoretical arguments that tort law is intellectually incoherent and unsystematic. As we saw in Ch.1, Cane would like to dismantle tort law and reconstruct it around a set of protected interests, providing a "system of ethical rules and principles of personal responsibility for conduct" (Cane, 1997, p.1). Street (see above, p.6) phrased this somewhat differently, asking the three basic questions:

- What interests does the law of torts protect?

- Against what general type of conduct—malicious, intentional, negligent, or accidental—are these interests protected?

- Is there some special circumstance that provides a defence?

We noted that these analyses did not allow the authors to move far from the laundry list of torts and, at the end of this short survey of tort law, our position is not much better. Half of tort law is still made up of a number of ancient actions, whose boundaries were settled in the distant past. The history of tort law since the Judicature Acts has largely consisted of efforts by the judiciary to reverse this situation. They have blurred the boundaries of the nominate torts with the aid of the overarching negligence principle, a process that started slowly, led up to *Donoghue* and picked up speed during the 1960s–70s, after *Hedley Byrne* and the *Dorset Yacht* case. Not only did the ambit of tort law widen exponentially but its style also changed dramatically. It began to evolve from a "law of torts", composed of a heterogeneous miscellany of causes of action with little or no connecting thread, towards a "law of tort", based on negligence as a general principle of civil liability.

In some areas of tort law, the process of evolution and development has proceeded faster and more effectively than in others. Since *Donoghue* gave the empire of contract its first shock, for example, the rules of contract and tort have become hopelessly intertwined and difficult to unravel. New challenges arise and are not always met successfully. We saw, for example, that the Human Rights Act has intensified problems over the controversial right to privacy and opened up a more general and still more controversial question as to whether violations of human rights should give rise to a right of damages for individuals. Whether the courts will be able to devise solutions for major problems of this kind is a very moot point. Yet Parliament, as we have seen, has intervened only very sporadically, usually to dispose of an inconvenient precedent or to stick a tiny patch on the worn fabric of tort law. The Law Commission has never been asked to undertake a thorough study of the subject, and many of its smaller studies—notably the programme on damages—have never been implemented or only partially. The same is true of the Report of the Pearson Commission (1978), the only comprehensive study of personal injuries litigation. As the pace of change has accelerated significantly, so has the function of government in policymaking and legislation expanded. In these circumstances, the judiciary clearly doubts both its capacity to move tort law forward in areas such as economic loss, which involve difficult policy issues, and the wisdom and legitimacy of so doing. These doubts are expressed in several common law countries by a reversion to "incrementalism", which undoubtedly expresses these judicial concerns.

During the course of this study, we have encountered principles akin to the flexible negligence principle that could be used for purposes of simplification. The most obvious of these principles is the principle of *Wilkinson*, first set out in Ch.1. This surfaced again in Ch.6, as articulated by Bowen L.J. in *Mogul v McGregor* (1889) that

"intentionally to do that which is calculated in the ordinary course of events to damage, and which does in fact damage, another in that person's property or trade is actionable if done without just cause or excuse."

This principle, which we called the *prima facie* tort doctrine, could apply to all intentional and malicious wrongdoing. In much the same way as Street suggests, it would mirror *Donoghue* in the field of negligence. Another principle considered in this book is the rule in *Rylands* (see above, p.87). This, we saw, could be used in areas appropriate for strict liability.

A move to this type of principled conceptual reasoning would undoubtedly help to make tort law less inscrutable and erratic. It might also halt the tendency to override existing torts by negligence. It would not, however, deal with the questions of which interests tort law should protect. These are questions of policy, for the resolution of which the intervention of the legislature, or in some cases, the European Union, is essential. Some of the issues, notably that of environmental protection—where judges are notably unwilling to get involved, as seen in Ch.5—combine scientific complexity with political sensitivity and need advice and attention from specialised agencies. Others involve the issue of insurance, which, as we saw in Ch.1, props up the tort system but is largely unacknowledged.

The silence in which this thorny topic has traditionally been shrouded may be disappearing. The press is full of reports of professionals moving out of risky professions, notably surgery and obstetrics, through inability to afford insurance cover. The Law Society, the Institute of Chartered Accountants, the Royal Institute of British Architects and the British Medical Association have all in recent years reported independently that their members have either failed to find insurers or can no longer afford the heavy premiums demanded. There is a serious danger that small businesses may go out of business and they are demanding a cap on professional negligence liability. So are other professions under similar pressure, notably the Big Four accountancy firms in respect of audit work in the aftermath of Enron. Directors' duties of care have grown enough to affect recruitment of non-executive directors, prompting government to relax the present law, which prohibits exemption and indemnity. In 1986, the Guardian Royal Exchange Insurance Company was refusing to handle new professional insurance business, having paid out more than £40 million in claims against accountants during 1985. In 1992 we saw the collapse of the Municipal Mutual Insurance, which insured 90 per cent of the country's local authorities. We read of the closure of children's playgrounds; cancellation of amateur art exhibitions; closing down of swimming baths and sports facilities; withdrawal of adventure holidays and school trips; and so on.

Whether or not they actually have this effect, cases like *Watson v British Boxing Board of Control* (2001) or *Vowles v Evans* (2003), which suddenly expand the liability of referees and those who organise sporting activities, are widely perceived as accentuating the problem.

As it was in the far-off days of Lord Campbell and the Fatal Accident Acts (see above, p.11), tort law is becoming a political issue. It is seen as an area in need of regulation, in which progress can only be made with support and a policy steer from government. The Australian Federal Government, faced with a sharp hike in insurance premiums and the collapse of two major public sector insurers, recently embarked on just such an inquiry. Concerned that the cost of insurance and the difficulty in obtaining it was beginning to have a serious "freezing effect" on the life of the community, it set up an advisory panel to review the law of negligence. In sharp contrast to the lengthy inquiry undertaken by the Pearson Commission and the Law Commission programme of painstaking reports on the law of damages, the Australian Ipp Committee was asked to work in a time frame of around two months. Its terms of reference were limited: to inquire into "the application, effectiveness and operation" of common law principles in personal injuries cases and "develop and evaluate principled options to limit liability and quantum of awards for damages". What emerged was a short policy document identifying areas where the law was supposedly having serious effects of "negative deterrence" (Ipp, 2002). Some changes to the principles of negligence were recommended: for example, the foreseeability test was to be pared down and a "negligence calculus" introduced, setting out a number of factors to be taken into consideration when the imposition of a duty of care is considered. The calculus, borrowed from the case law but integrated, requires the judge to weigh the seriousness and probability of harm against the burden of taking precautions and the social utility of the activity in question. Some areas of socially useful activity, such as sport and other recreational services, are immunised from excessive liability, as are the acts of rescuers and "good Samaritans", such as doctors who stop to help at an accident. These changes are not substantial but they serve to establish guidelines, pointing the courts in the direction that government wishes them to take. More importantly, damages have in some instances been pegged and, more influential still, lawyers' fees have been capped. Many of the changes have already been incorporated into legislation.

Over the last 10 years, the United Kingdom Government has instigated a major overhaul of English civil procedure (Woolf,

1996). More could still be done through arbitration and alternative dispute resolution to move personal injuries litigation in the direction of cheap and speedy outcomes. Administrative compensation schemes undoubtedly have a much greater part to play. Perhaps we should not complain that the life of tort law has not shown itself to be outstandingly logical or tidy; perhaps the search for coherence in law is no more than an academic dream and obsession. Reviewing two "obituaries of tort law", Ripstein (1998, pp.573–574) thought that it owed its long life to the fact that it "gives expression to a set of familiar and intuitively compelling ideas about responsibility and justice". For this reason alone, tort law is likely to survive. It is, however, time to follow Australia and move the reform process into the substance of tort law.

BIBLIOGRAPHY

Abel, R. (1982) "Torts" in *The Politics of Law, A Progressive Critique* (Kairys ed., New York, Pantheon)

Abel, R. (1994) *Speech and Respect* (London, Stevens)

Adams, J. and Brownsword, R. (2004) *Understanding Contract Law* (4th ed., London, Sweet & Maxwell)

Allen, D., Bourne, C. and Holyoak, J. (eds) (1979) *Accident Compensation after Pearson* (London, Sweet & Maxwell)

Andenas, M. and Fairgrieve, D. (2002) "Misfeasance in Public Office, Governmental Liability and European Influences" 51 *International and Comparative Law Quarterly* 757

Atiyah, P.S. (1970) *Accidents, Compensation and the Law* (London, Weidenfeld and Nicolson). And see Cane, P. (1999).

Atiyah, P.S. (1978) "Contracts, Promises and the Law of Obligations" 94 *Law Quarterly Review* 193

Atiyah, P.S. (1987a) "American Tort Law in Crisis" 7 *Oxford Journal of Legal Studies* 279

Atiyah, P.S. (1987b) *Pragmatism and Theory in English Law* (London, Stevens)

Atiyah, P.S. (1997) *The Damages Lottery* (Oxford, Hart Publishing)

Baldwin, R. (1987) "Health and Safety at Work: Consensus and Self-Regulation" in *Regulation and Public Law* (Baldwin and McCrudden ed., London, Weidenfeld and Nicolson)

Ballantine, A.A. (1916) "A Compensation Plan for Railway Accident Claims" 29 *Harvard Law Review* 705

Barendt, E. (1993) "Libel and Freedom of Speech in English Law" [1993] *Public Law* 449

Bingham, Lord (1996) "Opinion: Should There Be a Law to Protect Rights of Personal Privacy?" [1996] *European Human Rights Law Review* 450

Bingham, Lord (1998) "Tort and Human Rights" in *The Law of Obligations: Essays in Celebration of John Fleming* (Cane and Stapleton ed., Oxford, Clarendon)

Bishop, W. (1982) "Economic Loss in Tort" 2 *Oxford Journal of Legal Studies* 1

Blackstone, Sir W. (1787) *Commentaries on the Laws of England* (10th ed., London)

Brenner, J. (1973) "Nuisance Law and the Industrial Revolution" 3 *Journal of Legal Studies* 403

Bridgeman, J. and Jones, M. (1994) "Harassing Conduct and Outrageous Acts: A Cause of Action for Intentionally Inflicted Mental Distress?" 14 *Legal Studies* 180

Brownsword, R. (2003) "An Interest in Human Dignity as the Basis for Genomic Torts" 42 *Washburn Law Journal* 413

Buckley, R. (2002) "Nuisance and the Public Interest" 118 *Law Quarterly Review* 508

Calabresi, G. (1961) "Some Thoughts on Risk Distribution and the Law of Torts" 70 *Yale Law Journal* 499

Calabresi, G. (1970) *The Cost of Accidents* (New Haven, Yale University Press)

Calcutt, D. (1990) *Report of the Committee on Privacy and Related Matters*, Cm.1102 (London, HMSO)

Calcutt, D. (1993) *Review of Press Self-Regulation*, Cm.2135 (London, HMSO)

Cane, P. and Stapleton, J. (eds) (1998) *The Law of Obligations: Essays in Celebration of John Fleming* (Oxford, Clarendon)

Cane, P. (1982) "Justice and Justifications For Tort Liability" 2 *Oxford Journal of Legal Studies* 30

Cane, P. (1986) *An Introduction to Administrative Law* (2nd ed., Oxford, Clarendon)

Cane, P. (1996) *Tort Law and Economic Interests* (2nd ed., Oxford, Clarendon)

Cane, P. (1997) *An Anatomy of Tort Law* (Oxford, Hart Publishing)

Cane, P. (1999) "Damages in Public Law" 9 *University of Otago Law Review* 489

Cane, P. (1999) *Atiyah's Accidents, Compensation and the Law* (6th ed., London, Butterworths)

Carty, H. (1988) "Intentional Violations of Economic Interests: The Limits of Common Law Liability" 104 *Law Quarterly Review* 250

Cohen, D. (1993) "Tort Law and the Crown: Administrative Compensation and the Modern State" in *Tort Theory* (Cooper-Stephenson and Gibson ed., York, Captus University Publications)

Cm.962 (1989–90), *see* Taylor

Cm.394 , *see* Lord Chancellor's Department

Cm.1102 (1990), *see* Calcutt

Cm.2135 (1993), *see* Calcutt

Cm.2462 (1999), *see* MacPherson

Cmnd.5012 (1972), *see* Younger

Cmnd.5909 (1975), *see* Faulks

Cmnd.6428 (1976), *see* Law Commission

Cmnd.7054 (1978), *see* Pearson

Cmnd.9710 (1986), *see* Popplewell

Cmnd.9390 (1984), *see* Law Commission

Cm.4262–I (1999), *see* Macpherson

Conaghan, J. (1993) "Harassment and the Law of Torts" 1 *Feminist Legal Studies* 189

Conaghan, J. (1998) "Tort Litigation in the Context of Intra-Familial Abuse" 61 *Modern Law Review* 132

Conaghan, J. and Mansell, W. (1993) *The Wrongs of Tort* (2nd ed., London, Pluto Press)

Corfield, P. (1984) "Private Insurance" in *Compensation and Support for Illness and Injury* (Harris *et al.* ed., Oxford, Clarendon)

Craig, P. (1978) "Negligence in the Exercise of a Statutory Power" 94 *Law Quarterly Review* 428

Craig, P. (1993) "*Francovich*, Remedies and the Scope of Damages Liability" 109 *Law Quarterly Review* 595

Craig, P. and Fairgrieve, D. (1999) "Barrett, Negligence and Discretionary Powers" [1999] *Public Law* 626

Davies, M. (1981) "The Road from Morocco: *Polemis* Through *Donoghue* to No Fault" 45 *Modern Law Review* 534

Davies, M. (1989) "The End of the Affair: Duty of Care and Liability Insurance" 9 *Legal Studies* 67

Deakin, S., Johnston, A. and Markesinis, B. (2003) *Markesinis and Deakin's Tort Law* (5th ed., Oxford, Clarendon)

Dewes, D. and Trebilcock, M. (1992) "The Efficacy of the Tort System and its Alternatives: A Review of the Empirical Evidence" 30 *Osgoode Hall Law Journal* 57

Dewes, D., Duff, D. and Trebilcock, M. (1996) *Exploring the Domain of Accident Law: Taking the Facts Seriously* (Oxford and New York, Oxford University Press)

Dicey, A.V. (1885) *Introduction to the Law of the Constitution* (10th ed. E.C.S. Wade, London, Macmillan, 1959, repr. 1973)

Donaldson, L. (2003) *Making Amends: A Consultation Paper Setting Out Proposals for Reforming the Approach to Clinical Negligence in the NHS* (London, Department of Health)

Duff, P. (1998) "The Measure of Criminal Injuries Compensation: Political Pragmatism or Dog's Dinner?" 18(1) *Oxford Journal of Legal Studies* 105

Dworkin, G. (1979) "Compensation and Payments for Vaccine Damage" *Journal of Social Welfare Law* 330

Englard, J. (1980) "The System Builders: A Critical Appraisal of Modern American Tort Theory" 9 *Journal of Legal Studies* 27

Epstein, B. (1973) "A Theory of Strict Liability" 2 *Journal of Legal Studies* 151

Evans, R. (1982) "Damages for Unlawful Administrative Action: The Remedy for Misfeasance in Public Office" 31 *International and Comparative Law Quarterly* 640

Fagelson, I. (1979) "The Last Bastion of Fault? Contributory Negligence in Actions for Employer's Liability" 42 *Modern Law Review* 646

Fairgrieve, D. (2002) *State Liability in Tort* (Oxford, Oxford University Press)

Faulks Committee (1975) *Report of the Committee on Defamation*, Cmnd.5909

Feldman, D. (1999) "Human Dignity as a Legal Value" [1999] *Public Law* 682

Feldthusen, B. (1996) "The Recovery of Pure Economic Loss in Canada: Proximity, Justice, Rationality and Chaos" 24 *Manitoba Law Journal* 1

Ferguson, J. (2003) "Medical Misadventure under Accident Compensation: Diagnosis and Treatment of a Problem?" [2003] *New Zealand Law Review* 485

Fifoot, C. (1949) *History and Sources of the Common Law, Tort and Contract* (London, Stevens)

Fleming, J. (1984) "Is There a Future for Tort?" 58 *Australian Law Journal* 131

Fleming, J. (1987) *The American Tort Process* (Oxford, Clarendon)

Fleming, J. (1992) "Once More—Economic Loss" 12 *Oxford Journal of Legal Studies* 558

Friedmann, W. (1949) "Social Insurance and the Principles of Tort Liability" 63 *Harvard Law Review* 241

Friedmann, W. (1971) *Law in a Changing Society* (Harmondsworth, Pelican)

Goodhart, A. (1953) *English Law and the Moral Law* (London, Stevens)

Green, L. (1953) "The Individual's Protection under Negligence Law: Risk Sharing" 47 *Northwestern University Law Review* 751

Gregory, C. (1951) "Trespass to Negligence to Absolute Liability" 37 *Virginia Law Review* 359

Gutteridge (1906) "Abuse of Rights" 5 *Cambridge Law Journal* 22

Halliday, T. and Karpik, L. (1997) *Lawyers and the Rise of Western Political Liberalism* (Oxford, Clarendon)

Harlow, C. (1984) "A Treatise For Our Times?" 47 *Modern Law Review* 487

Harlow, C. (2004) *State Liability: Tort Law and Beyond* (Oxford, Oxford University Press)

Harris, D. (1974) "Accident Compensation in New Zealand: A Comprehensive Insurance System" 37 *Modern Law Review* 361

Harris, D. *et al.* (1984) *Compensation and Support for Illness and Injury* (Oxford, Clarendon)

Harris, D. (1991a) "Evaluating the Goals of Personal Injury Law: Some Empirical Evidence" in *Essays in Honour of Patrick Atiyah* (Cane and Stapleton ed., Oxford, Clarendon)

Harris, D. (1991b) "Tort Law Reform in the United States" 11 *Oxford Journal of Legal Studies* 407

Hedley, S. (1994) "Group Personal Injury Litigation and Public Opinion" 14 *Legal Studies* 70

Hensler, J. (2002) "As Time Goes By: Asbestos Litigation After *Amchem* and *Ortiz*" [2002] *Texas Law Review* 1899

Hepple, B., Howarth, D. and Matthews, M. (2000) *Tort Cases and Materials* (5th ed., London, Butterworths)

Hogg, P. (1989) *Liability of the Crown* (2nd ed., Toronto, Carswell)

Holmes, O.W. (1906) *The Common Law* (Boston, Little, Brown and Co, Mark de Wolfe ed., 1973)

Holmes, O.W. (1894) "Privilege, Malice and Intent" 8 *Harvard Law Review* 1

Holyoak, J. (1983) "Tort and Contract after *Junior Books*" 99 *Law Quarterly Review* 591

Huber, P. (1988) *Liability, the Legal Revolution and its Consequences* (New York, Basic Books)

Hutchinson, A. and Morgan, D. (1984), "The Canengusian Connection: A Kaleidoscope of Tort Theory" 22 *Osgoode Hall Law Journal* 69

Ipp, D. (2002) *Review of the Law of Negligence* (Canberra, Commonwealth of Australia)

Isscharoff, S. (2002) "'Shocked': Mass Torts and Aggregate Asbestos Litigation After *Amchem* and *Ortiz*" 80 *Texas Law Review* 1

Ison, T. (1967) *The Forensic Lottery* (London, Staples Press)

Ison, T. (1993) "Changes to the Accident Compensation System: An International Perspective" 23 *Victoria University of Wellington Law Review* 26

Jaffey, J.E. (1984) "Contract in Tort's Clothing" [1984] *Legal Studies* 77

Jowell, J. (2000) "The Rule of Law Today" in *The Changing Constitution* (4th ed., Jowell and Oliver ed., Oxford, Clarendon)

Kidner, R. (1983) "Resiling from the *Anns* Principle: The Variable Nature of Proximity in Negligence" 7 *Legal Studies* 319

Klar, L.N. (1983) "New Zealand's Accident Compensation Scheme: A Tort Lawyer's Perspective" in *Issues in Tort Law* (Steel and Rodgers-Magnet ed., Toronto, Carswell)

Kötz, H. (1987) "Taking Civil Codes Less Seriously" 50 *Modern Law Review* 1

Law Commission (1967) *Civil Liability for Animals* (Law Com.13)

Law Commission (1970) *Report on Civil Liability for Dangerous Things and Activities* (Law Com.32)

Law Commission (1976) *Report on Liability for Damage or Injury to Trespassers and Related Questions of Occupiers Liability Law*, Cmnd.6428

Law Commission (1993) *Aggravated, Exemplary and Restitutionary Damages*, Law Com.132

Law Commission (1997a) *Aggravated, Exemplary and Restitutionary Damages*, Law Com.247

Law Commission (1997b) *Limitation of Actions*, Law Com.151

Law Commission (1998) *Liability for Psychiatric Illness*, Law Com.249

Law Commission (1999) *Report on Damages for Personal Injury: Non-Pecuniary Loss*, Law Com.257

Lewis, R. (1993) "Health Authorities and the Payment of Damages by Means of a Pension" 56 *Modern Law Review* 844

Linden, A. (1969) "Is Tort Law Relevant to the Automobile Accident Compensation Problem?" 47 *Texas Law Review* 1012

Linden, A. (1973) "Tort Law as Ombudsman" 51 *Canadian Bar Review* 155

Linden, A. (1983) "Reconsidering Tort Law as Ombudsman" in *Issues in Tort Law* (Steel and Rodgers-Magnet ed., Toronto, Carswell)

Loveland, I. (1994) "Defamation of 'Government': Taking Lessons From America?" 14 *Legal Studies* 206

Loveland, I. (2000) "*Reynolds v Times Newspapers* in the House of Lords" [2000] *Public Law* 351

Lunney, M. (1995) "What Price a Chance?" 15 *Legal Studies* 1

Luntz, H. (1996) "Mrs Whitaker's Gothic Cathedral" 4 *Torts Law Journal* 195

Luntz, H. (1998) "Liability of Statutory Authority for Omissions" 6 *Torts Law Journal* 107

McGrath, M. (1985) "The Recovery of Pure Economic Loss in Negligence—An Emerging Dichotomy" 5 *Oxford Journal of Legal Studies* 350

McKendrick, E. (1990) "Vicarious Liability and Independent Contractors—A Re-Examination" 53 *Modern Law Review* 770

McLachlin J. (1998) "Negligence Law—Proving the Connection" in *Torts Tomorrow: A Tribute to John Fleming* (Mullany and Linden ed., Sydney, LBC Information Services)

McLaren, J. (1983) "Nuisance Law and the Industrial Revolution: Some Lessons from Social History" (1983) 3 *Oxford Journal of Legal Studies* 155

McLean, H. (1998) "Negligent Regulatory Authorities and the Duty of Care" 18 *Oxford Journal of Legal Studies* 442

Macpherson, Sir W. (1999) *The Stephen Lawrence Inquiry*, Cm.4262–I

Markesinis, B.S. (1989) "Negligence, Nuisance and Affirmative Duties of Action" 105 *Law Quarterly Review* 104

Markesinis, B. (1990) "Our Patchy Law of Privacy—Time to Do Something About It" 53 *Modern Law Review* 802

Markesinis, B.S. and Deakin, S. (1992) "The Random Element of Their Lordships' Infallible Judgement: An Economic and Comparative Analysis of the Tort of Negligence from *Anns* to *Murphy*" 55 *Modern Law Review* 561

Mason, A. (1998) "Human Rights and the Law of Torts" in *The Law of Obligations: Essays in Celebration of John Fleming* (Cane and Stapleton ed., Oxford, Clarendon Press)

Morgan, J. (2003) "Lost Causes in the House of Lords: *Fairchild v Glenhaven Funeral Services*" 66 *Modern Law Review* 277

Morgan, J. (2004) "Tort, Insurance and Incoherence" 67 *Modern Law Review* 384

Morris, A. (1995) "On the Normative Foundations of Indirect Discrimination Law: Understanding the Competing Models of Discrimination Law as Aristotelian Forms of Justice" 15 *Oxford Journal of Legal Studies* 199

Mowbray, A. (2001) *Cases and Materials on the European Convention on Human Rights* (London, Butterworths)

Mullany, N. and Handford P. (1993) *Tort Liability for Psychiatric Damage: The Law of Nervous Shock* (Sydney, The Law Book Co)

Murphy, J. (1999) "Formularism and Tort Law" 21 *Adelaide Law Review* 115

National Audit Office (2002–03) *Ministry of Defence: Compensation Claims* (HC 957)

Newark, F.M. (1949) "The Boundaries of Nuisance" 65 *Law Quarterly Review* 480

Newark, F.M. (1961) "Non-Natural User and *Rylands v Fletcher*" 24 *Modern Law Review* 557

Newdick, C. (1985) "Strict Liability for Defective Drugs in the Pharmaceutical Industry" 101 *Law Quarterly Review* 405

Ogus, A. and Richardson, G. (1977) "Economics and the Environment: A Study of Private Nuisance" [1977] *Cambridge Law Journal* 284

Pearson, Lord (1978) *Report of the Royal Commission on Civil Liability for Personal Injuries*, Cmnd.7054

Perry, S. (1993) "Loss, Agency and Responsibility for Outcomes: Three Conceptions of Corrective Justice" in *Tort Theory* (Cooper-Stephenson and Gibson ed., York, Captus University Publications)

Philips (1981) *Report of the Royal Commission on Criminal Procedure*, Cmnd.8092

Philipson, G. (2003) "Transforming Breach of Confidence: Towards a Common Law Right of Privacy under the Human Rights Act" 66 *Modern Law Review* 726

Pilkington, M. (1984) "Damages as a Remedy for Infringement of the Canadian Charter of Rights and Freedoms" 62 *Canadian Bar Review* 517

Pipe, G. (1994) "Exemplary Damages After Camelford" 57 *Modern Law Review* 91

Pollock, F. (1887) *Law of Torts* (London, Stevens)

Pollock, F. (1931) "Book Review" 47 *Law Quarterly Review* 588

Popplewell, (1986) *Final Report of the Inquiry into TITLE???*, Cmnd.9710

Posner, R. (1973) "A Theory of Negligence" 1 *Journal of Legal Studies* 29

Posner, R. (1992) *Economic Analysis of Law* (5th ed., Little Brown, Boston)

Prescott, P. (1991) "*Kaye v Robertson*—A Reply" 54 *Modern Law Review* 451

Prevett, J.H. (1972) "The Actuarial Assessment of Damages" 35 *Modern Law Review* 140, 257

Priest, G. (1985) "The Invention of Enterprise Liability: A Critical History of the Intellectual Foundations of Modern Tort Law" 14 *Journal of Legal Studies* 461

Prosser, W. (1960) "The Assault on the Citadel (Strict Liability to the Consumer)" 69 *Yale Law Journal* 1099

Prosser, W. (1966) "The Fall of the Citadel (Strict Liability to the Consumer)" 50 *Minnesota Law Review* 791

Rand (1987) "Trends in Tort Litigation: The Story Behind the Statistics" (Santa Monica, Institute for Civil Justice)

Reece, H. (1995) "Loss of Chances in the Law" 59 *Modern Law Review* 188

Ripstein, A. (1998) "Some Recent Obituaries of Tort Law" 48 *University of Toronto Law Journal* 561

Robens (1972) *Report of the Robens Committee*

Robertson, G. (1983) "The Law Commission on Criminal Libel" [1983] *Public Law* 208

Rosenberg, D. (1984) "The Causal Connection in Mass Exposure Cases: A Public Law Vision of the Tort System" 97 *Harvard Law Review* 851

Ross, M. (1993) "After *Francovitch*" 56 *Modern Law Review* 55

Rubinstein, M. (1972) *Wicked, Wicked Libels* (London, Routledge & Kegan Paul)

Salmond and Heuston (1992) *The Law of Torts* (10th ed., Heuston and Chambers ed., London, Sweet & Maxwell)

Schwartz, G. (1982) "Deterrence and Punishment in the Common Law of Punitive Damages: A Comment" 56 *Southern California Law Review* 133

Schwartz, G. (1992) "The Beginning and the Possible End of the Rise of Modern American Tort Law" 26 *Georgia Law Review* 601

Schuck, P. (1983) *Suing Government: Citizen Remedies for Official Wrongs* (New Haven, Yale University Press)

Schuck, P. (1986) *Agent Orange on Trial* (Cambridge, Mass., Bellknop Press of Harvard University Press)

Schuck, P. (1988) "The New Ideology of Tort Law" 92 *The Public Interest* 93

Scraton, P. (1992) "Justice: Hillsborough's Final Victim?" [1992] *Legal Action*, April, 7

Select Committee on Culture, Media and Sport (2002–03) *Privacy and Media Intrusion*, HC 458

Smith, J. and Burns, P. (1983) "*Donoghue v Stevenson*—The Not So Golden Anniversary" 46 *Modern Law Review* 147

Spigelman, J. "Negligence: The Last Outpost of the Welfare State" (2002) 76 *Australian Law Journal* 432

Spigelman, J. (2004) "Tort Law Reform in Australia" (unpublished lecture)

Stapleton, J. (1988) "The Gist of Negligence" 104 *Law Quarterly Review* 213 and 389

Stapleton, J. (1994) "In Restraint of Tort" in *The Frontiers of Liability III* (Birks ed., Oxford, Clarendon)

Stapleton, J. (1995a) "Tort, Insurance and Ideology" 58 *Modern Law Review* 820

Stapleton, J. (1995b) "Duty of Care: Peripheral Parties and Alternative Opportunities for Deterrence" 111 *Law Quarterly Review* 301

Stapleton, J. (2001) "Unpacking Causation" in *Relating to Responsibility* (Cane and Gardner ed., Oxford, Hart Publishing)

Stapleton, J. (2002) "Lords a'Leaping Evidentiary Gaps" 10 *Torts Law Journal* 376

Steele, J. (1995) "Private Law and the Environment: Nuisance in Context" 15 *Legal Studies* 236

Steele, J. and Wikeley, N. (1997) "Dust on the Streets and Liability for Environmental Cancers" 60 *Modern Law Review* 265

Street, H. (1983) *Street on Torts* (London, Butterworths)

Sugarman, D. (1986) "Legal Theory, the Common Law Mind and the Making of the Textbook Tradition" in *Legal Theory and the Common Law* (Twining ed., Oxford, Basil Blackwell)

Sugarman, S. (2000) "A Century of Change in Personal Injuries Law" 88 *California Law Review* 2403

Taylor, Lord Justice (1989) *Final Report of the Inquiry into the Hillsborough Stadium Disaster*, Cm.962 (1989–90)

Tunc, A. (1972) "Tort Law and the Moral Law" 30 *Cambridge Law Journal* 247

van Gerven, W. *et al.*, (1998) *Cases, Materials and Text on National, Supernational and International Tort Law, Scope of Protection* (Oxford, Hart Publishing)

Veljanovski, C. (1990) *The Economics of Law—An Introductory Text* (London, Institute of Economic Affairs)

Vickery, A. (1982) "Breach of Confidence: An Emerging Tort" 82 *Columbia Law Review* 1426

Walford, R. (2002) "Liability of Professionals to Non-Clients" [2002] *Professional Negligence* 177

Warren, S. and Brandeis, L. (1890) "The Right to Privacy" 4 *Harvard Law Review* 193

Weinrib, E. (1989) "Understanding Tort Law" 23 *Valparaiso University Law Review* 485

Weinrib, E. (1995) *The Idea of Private Law* (Cambridge, Mass., Harvard University Press)

White, E. (1980) *Tort Law in America: An Intellectual History* (Oxford, Oxford University Press)

Wilkinson, D. (1994) *"Cambridge Water Company v Eastern Counties Leather plc*: Diluting Liability for Continuing Escapes" 57 *Modern Law Review* 799

Williams, Glanville (1960) "The Effect of Penal Legislation in the Law of Tort" 23 *Modern Law Review* 233

Winfield, P. (1926) "The Myth of Absolute Liability" 42 *Law Quarterly Review* 37

Winfield, P. (1931a) "The Right to Privacy" 47 *Law Quarterly Review* 23

Winfield, P. (1931b) *Province of the Law of Tort* (Cambridge, Cambridge University Press)

Winfield, P. (1934) "Duty in Tortious Negligence" 34 *Columbia Law Review* 41

Winfield, P. and Jolowicz, T. (2002) *Winfield and Jolowicz on Tort* (16th ed., W.V.H. Rogers)

Witt, J. (2003) "Speedy Fred Taylor and the Ironies of Enterprise Liability" 193 *Columbia Law Review* 1

Woodhouse (1967) *Report of the Royal Commission of Inquiry into Compensation for Personal Injury in New Zealand*

Woolf, Lord (1996) *Access to Justice, Final Report to the Lord Chancellor on the Civil Justice System in England and Wales* (London, Lord Chancellor's Department)

Woolf, Lord (2000) "The Human Rights Act and Remedies" in *Judicial Review in an International Perspective* (Andenas and Fairgrieve ed., London, Kluwer Law International)

Wright, C. (1942) "Introduction to the Law of Torts" 8 *Cambridge Law Journal* 238

Younger, K. (1972) *Report of the Committee on Privacy*, Cmnd.5012

TABLE OF CASES

INDEX